TECHNOLOGY OF THE
CHAMP CAR

TECHNOLOGY OF THE CHAMP CAR

Nigel Macknight

HAZLETON PUBLISHING

publisher
RICHARD POULTER

....

production manager
STEVEN PALMER

....

managing editor
PETER LOVERING

....

publishing development manager
SIMON MAURICE

....

business development manager
SIMON SANDERSON

....

sales promotion
CLARE KRISTENSEN

....

art editor
STEVE SMALL

....

photography by
GLYN BARNEY
MICHAEL C. BROWN
with additional contributions by
AEROTECH
ALLSPORT
AP RACING
KEVIN CHEVIS
HEXCEL COMPOSITES
ILMOR ENGINEERING
REYNARD RACING CARS
T.C. ALLEN/PHOTOSPHERE
BRYN WILLIAMS

First published in 1998

ISBN 1-874557-92-6

Acknowledgements

For their co-operation in the research for this book, many thanks to: Simon Ellis of AP Racing; Patrick Peal of Band & Brown; Tony Harrison and Barry Wainwright of Brookhouse Paxford; T.E. McHale of CART; Dick Jones of Cranfield Impact Centre; Steve Orlando of Goodyear Racing; Natasha Spreckley, Mario Illien and Alan Cook of Ilmor Engineering; Roger Tyler and Colin Whittamore of Lola Cars International; Nick Goozée, Sharon Hickey, David Johnson-Newell and John Travis of Penske Cars; Scott Mitchell of Pi Research; Alison Hill and Barry Ward of Reynard Racing Cars; and Steve Gold and Derrick Worthington of Xtrac.

Printed in Hong Kong through World Print

distributors

UNITED KINGDOM	NORTH AMERICA	AUSTRALIA	NEW ZEALAND	SOUTH AFRICA
Biblios Ltd	Motorbooks International	Technical Book and Magazine	David Bateman Ltd	Motorbooks
Star Road	PO Box 1, 729 Prospect Ave.	Co. Pty	PO Box 100-242	341 Jan Smuts Avenue
Partridge Green	Osceola	295 Swanston Street	North Shore Mail Centre	Craighall Park
West Sussex RH13 8LD	Wisconsin 54020, USA	Melbourne, Victoria 3000	Auckland 1330	Johannesburg
Tel: 01403 710971	Tel: (1) 715 294 3345	Tel: (03) 9663 3951	Tel: (9) 415 7664	Tel: (011) 325 4458/60
Fax: 01403 711143	Fax: (1) 715 294 4448	Fax: (03) 9663 2094	Fax: (9) 415 8892	Fax: (011) 325 4146

CONTENTS

introduction

DEFINING THE CONCEPT

THE governing body for Champ Car racing is Championship Auto Racing Teams (CART) Inc., which was established as a corporation in the State of Michigan in 1978. CART is a co-operative owned and run by the competitors themselves, and is currently under the presidency of Andrew Craig. Unlike the Formula 1 World Championship, in which competing teams are required to design and manufacture their own cars, teams contesting the CART FedEx Championship Series are free to purchase a proprietary chassis – and the vast majority do so, although many devote considerable resources to their own independent development programmes, focusing in particular on aerodynamic refinements and suspension evolution.

Champ Car racing is extremely competitive and entertaining, because so many drivers are in with a chance of winning. This is largely due to the fact that it is essentially a 'customer car' series in which many teams have near-identical equipment.

The Champ Car series is the oldest automobile racing championship in the world. The well-known 'Indy car' tag was dropped in an out-of-court settlement with the organisers of the breakaway Indy Racing League (IRL). The current CART FedEx Championship Series is actually four championships rolled into one. Like Formula 1, there is a Drivers' Championship running parallel to a Constructors' Championship for the chassis manufacturers. But Champ Car racing also has a Manufacturers' Cup, specifically for the engine manufacturers to contest, and there is a Nations' Cup for drivers, based on nationality.

This book is intended to illuminate the process by which Champ Car manufacturers create their cars – placing particular emphasis on racetrack action to illustrate the key principles.

A key difference between Champ Car racing and Formula 1 is the use of highly banked oval circuits – and, in particular, the 500-mile races run on two-mile ovals known as Superspeedways. Although there are some excellent road circuits and street circuits on the calendar, the spectacular Superspeedways – with their electrifying lap speeds – are synonymous with Champ Car racing in the eyes of the public.

As well as requiring a fundamentally different aerodynamic configuration and suspension set-up, Superspeedways place exceptional demands on the men at the wheel. Drivers who are otherwise licensed to compete in Champ Car races are not eligible to compete in 500-mile races unless they comply with additional requirements imposed by CART, including passing a more stringent driving proficiency test and physical examination.

All Champ Car races have rolling starts – a concession to safety – and another distinctive feature of Champ Car racing is the prevalence of 'the yellow flag'. While Formula 1 spectators are well familiar with rules requiring drivers to slow down, exercise caution and maintain their relative positions on a particular corner where there is a temporary hazard, and will also see the safety car emerge at least once in the course of a season to control the pace of the pack around the racetrack, in Champ Car racing such procedures are an integral part of the competition – and a key element in race strategy.

For this reason, a brief outline of the yellow flag regulations is appropriate.

After the yellow flag is displayed, the race leader must slow down to a pace car lap speed, while the rest of the field closes up behind it. The cars must not pass under a yellow flag. Instead, they must maintain station until it is withdrawn and the green flag or green light is again displayed, which will only happen once the field has closed up and the racetrack has been cleared.

At any point in this procedure, the pace car may join the racetrack to regulate the speed of the field. Whenever possible, competitors are given a one-lap notification that the pace car will be leaving the racetrack. At a prescribed location, the flashing light on the pace car is turned off and it veers away from the racing line to allow the pack to resume battle.

During races on road circuits, the yellow flag may also be displayed from particular flag stations around the racetrack to indicate a specific area of danger. A waving yellow flag in such areas indicates great danger and compels the drivers to reduce speed and be prepared to stop. The pace car is despatched at road circuits if the entire racetrack is under yellow. A 'full course yellow' condition prevails whenever it becomes necessary to despatch an ambulance onto the racetrack. Usually, two yellow flags are displayed at each flag station to indicate this condition.

Champ Cars are slightly larger, by regulation, than Formula 1 cars – and they are heavier. CART regulations dictate the form the cars will take to such an extent that they all look very similar. There are regulations governing the overall length of the cars, their width, their height, the dimensions of their aerodynamic appendages and the amount by which they overhang the front and rear wheels, and a great many other dimensional limitations – all policed by taking precise measurements from strategic positions (termed 'hard points') on the cars.

The minimum permissible length of a Champ Car is 482.6 cm (190 in), while the maximum permissible length is 497.8 cm (196 in) – just 152 mm (6 in) more. The minimum permissible width is 197.5 cm (77.75 in), while the maximum permissible width is 199.4 cm (78.5 in) – *less* than 25 mm (1 in) more – but that is only over the rear wheels. The bodywork and aerodynamic devices forward of the rear wheels must not be wider than 160 cm (63 in). The height of the car, measured from the lowest point of the bodywork or chassis to the highest point of the bodywork or aerodynamic devices, must not exceed 81.3 cm (32 in).

In addition to dimensional limitations, there are restrictions on the degree to which innovative technological solutions can be applied to the eternal conundrum of 'going faster'. For example, the use of composite materials as structural load-bearing components is limited to the chassis, the bodywork, and aerodynamic devices and their associated supporting structures. Therefore, the more widespread use of composite materials seen in Formula 1 – for suspension components and, more recently, gearbox casings – is not countenanced.

CART Stewards may order disassembly and inspection of any car at any time to ascertain its conformity with the rules.

A fundamental difference between Champ Car racing and Formula 1 from the regulatory standpoint is the fact that the rules tend not to be open to interpretation. Increasingly in Formula 1, the written regulations are 'fleshed out' by clarifications by the governing body – the Fédération Internationale de l'Automobile (FIA) – in response to specific proposals from car designers: the latter are obliged to ask when they wish to stray into a regulatory 'grey area' with a new innovation. The FIA feels that governing in this manner is the only realistic approach, because designers will always find a way around published rules. Champ Car racing has an entirely different culture – one in which competitors tend to keep to the spirit of the regulations. In any case, CART's regulations are framed in crystal-clear language, and limits on technology keep 'questionable' innovation in check.

The regulations effectively define the order in which the key elements of Champ Cars are laid out, front to back. Starting at the front, the driver's foot pedals must be a mandatory minimum distance behind the nosebox, for safety reasons. Working back from that, the fuel load must be stored entirely behind the driver, again for safety reasons. The engine and gearbox will inevitably be located behind the fuel, because there is nowhere else for them to go, so there is hardly any scope for a truly innovative chassis layout.

Even if the regulations were freer, the dimensions of some elements of the car cannot be significantly altered by *any* designer – most notably the dimensions of the cockpit, which must be generous enough to accommodate the driver in relative comfort and safety. Although car designers have some influence over engine design, there is a physical limit to how compact an engine of a given capacity can be. A gearbox, too – with all of its ratios to accommodate – can only be so small.

Although there are notable exceptions to the rule, the process of designing a new car tends to be evolutionary rather than revolutionary. There is a strong tendency to make an existing concept better, rather than to discard it totally and start over. In fact, a certain percentage of components are actually carried over from the previous year's car in the interests of reliability – particularly those components which have no direct impact on lap times: for example, components within the fuel system.

In years past, the skills of an exceptional driver could make up for the deficiencies of an improperly designed car, but that is no longer the case. The plain fact is, in Champ Car racing today, designers are as valuable as the men at the wheel – and as a consequence, they have become increasingly well paid.

In sharp contrast to earlier eras, when individual designers were credited with designing entire cars almost single-handedly, today's cars are designed by a large *team* of designers, due to the sheer complexity of the task. Nevertheless, there is usually one individual with over-riding governance of the essential concept who leads the others: for example, John Travis at Penske, and Malcolm Oastler at Reynard (pictured here). Others then play vital roles undertaking specific aspects of the design – aerodynamicists, composites engineers, transmission designers and so forth – and 'detail draughtsmen' assist the key individuals by fleshing out specific aspects of the design.

Finally, there are design personnel engaged almost exclusively in research and development work.

There are typically four phases in the design of a Champ Car: conceptual scheming, preliminary scheming, final scheming and detailing. Design activities are very much computer-based, with a wide range of software being employed throughout the process. There has been an almost total transition away from paper engineering drawings in favour of Computer-Aided Design (CAD) – so 'draughtsmanship' in its strictest sense has been supplanted by 'CAD modelling', in which shapes are generated entirely digitally and represented on-screen in either two-dimensional or quasi-3D form.

Formidable computer power then allows designers to manipulate the models at will. They can alter them when design changes are necessary, and can 'rotate' components to view them from an almost infinite number of perspectives, and in cross-section at any point (station) along their length.

Once the designer has input a design change, all of the necessary calculations and draughtsmanship are undertaken by the computer software, which presents the end result almost instantaneously – avoiding the time-consuming task of creating new sets of conventional paper drawings every time something is changed.

When a CAD system is linked to a group of machine tools, the capability is extended to become Computer-Aided Manufacture (CAM), allowing components which have been modelled on-screen to be partially or wholly manufactured virtually independent of human intervention – saving precious time, because machines can work around the clock without feeling the strain!

CART regulations stipulate that, for Superspeedway events, the minimum permissible weight of the car is 692.35 kg (1525 lb), while for other oval, road-circuit and street-circuit events it is 703.7 kg (1550 lb). The car's weight is measured without fuel, but with the coolant and lubricants in place. To verify that cars meet this requirement, technical inspectors frequently position them on four hyper-sensitive pressure pads to measure their weight with great accuracy.

Manufacturers are generally able to build their cars below the minimum weight limit, then add blocks of lead ballast to bring them back up to the required minimum – positioning the ballast so as to assist in achieving the desired weight distribution. The lead is placed low down, to help keep the car's centre of gravity as low as possible. Although CART permits ballast to be carried, provided it is fitted within the wheelbase and is declared to officials prior to the race, it urges competitors to keep ballast to a minimum and 'invest' as much of the weight quota as possible in the structure of the car, pointing out that the mandatory minimum weight limit is intended 'to encourage engineering and design practices and the selection of materials that will result in the production of structurally safe race cars'.

Achieving a low centre of gravity is a key objective in the design process, because it makes the car more stable under heavy cornering, braking and acceleration forces. The weight *distribution* is also critically important, because distributing the weight more evenly between the front and rear of the car allows both sets of tyres to contribute more effectively to the overall performance and handling. Designers attempt to bring weight forward as much as possible, because the car's heaviest components – the engine, the gearbox and the fuel load – are unavoidably concentrated at the rear, placing a proportionately greater burden on the rear tyres.

TECHNOLOGY OF THE CHAMP CAR

Above all other factors, the key to designing a successful Champ Car is achieving an excellent aerodynamic performance. Aerodynamic devices abound on the modern Champ Car. The most visible are the aerofoil surfaces mounted at the front and rear of the cars, which generate huge downforce and thus provide greater levels of grip in the corners. But there are other aerodynamic devices, almost hidden from view – in particular, the underbody, which works in conjunction with a system of 'tunnels' at the rear of the car – which generate even more downforce and grip.

Mechanical, as opposed to aerodynamic, grip is another vitally important quality. This derives from the car's weight distribution and suspension geometry, and the performance of the differential and the tyres.

Blending the aerodynamic and mechanical qualities into a winning package is the goal of all Champ Car designers.

chapter 1 THE CHASSIS

BECAUSE it generally takes the longest time to produce, the chassis is usually the first element of the car to have its design committed to manufacture. Champ Car chassis are produced almost entirely from composite materials: in this case, the term 'composite' means a combination of two skins of multi-ply carbonfibre sandwiching a layer of aluminium honeycomb. However, the term can also be applied to the carbonfibre itself, as it is a composite of the carbon fibres and a pre-impregnated epoxy resin.

Pre-impregnating the fibres ensures that the resin is evenly distributed, guaranteeing consistency in the quality and performance of the finished product once the resin has been hardened (cured) by the application of extreme heat and pressure.

To simplify production, the chassis is built in several pieces – known as panels – then bonded and riveted together. The largest panels are the upper and lower chassis halves: smaller panels include the rollover hoop, three internal bulkheads, and the (removable) nosebox.

Before the panels themselves can be produced, a full-sized pattern must be made for each panel. From these patterns, moulds are made, then the composite materials are laid up in the moulds to make the panels themselves.

A Champ Car chassis is structurally very complex, because the forces acting upon it are themselves extremely complex. This is not surprising, as the chassis is the central structural element of the car, with virtually all of the other load-bearing elements attached directly to it. There are powerful and wildly fluctuating forces being fed in through the front suspension as it responds to high cornering and braking forces, and absorbs bumps in the racetrack surface. There are massive bending loads being fed in at the engine mounts, and brutal twisting forces, too, because this is the structural joint where the front half of the car – the chassis itself – is attached to the rear half: the engine, gearbox, rear suspension and rear aerofoil assemblies, which are all fixed together to form a single structure.

Additional twisting forces are fed in at the engine mounts by the torque effect from the engine when the driver accelerates hard.

At the opposite end of the chassis, huge aerodynamic loads are fed in via the nosebox from the downforce generated by the front aerofoil assemblies. Substantial forces are also fed in from beneath the chassis – from downforce generated by the underbody – and from its flanks, from the airflow rushing over and through the sidepods.

The chassis even has loads imposed on it from within, because the G-forces from the driver's body are fed in from his seat and safety harness mountings.

To deal with such complex forces effectively, and contribute to the overall performance and handling of the car, a fundamental design objective is to create sufficient stiffness to prevent the chassis flexing. Here, the requirement is for both torsional stiffness (a resistance to twisting loads) and beam stiffness (a resistance to either lateral or longitudinal bending loads). Another fundamental design objective is to create sufficient impact resistance: the chassis should be resilient enough to protect the driver in the event of an accident – and must be proved to be so to CART's satisfaction.

There is a potential conflict between the need for stiffness and the need for impact resistance – because with any carbonfibre material, the more stiffness it offers, the less resilience it has. This conflict can be partly resolved by creating a smoothly flowing chassis shape which spreads impact loads evenly, rather than introducing sharp corners which concentrate them.

Unlike Formula 1, where the crashworthiness of the cars is verified in an extensive series of crash tests, the crashworthiness of Champ Cars is assured by stringent construction specifications laid down by CART – although there are *some* mandatory crash tests, all of which are detailed in the next chapter.

CART places restrictions on the types of carbonfibre which may be used. So-called high modulus carbonfibres are outlawed because they tend to be so stiff that they become brittle. CART also specifies minimum wall thicknesses for critical parts of the chassis, and its regulations require manufacturers to maintain detailed records of all of the materials and processes employed in the construction of the chassis, so that every element of its structure can be traced back to its origins if any doubts arise about its integrity or compliance. Even repairs must be documented.

Chassis manufacturers must issue a certificate to the team owner, and to CART itself, certifying that all of the required manufacturing processes and testing have been properly and successfully completed on each and every chassis.

The chassis's inner and outer carbonfibre skins are each typically composed of between five and seven layers of varying material thicknesses and types, but in regions where greater strength and/or rigidity are required there might be as many as several dozen layers.

By laying up the individual pieces of carbonfibre so that their fibres are oriented in particular directions, it is possible to transfer loads to specific parts of the structure, or to dissipate them over a wider area. For example, it may be desirable to transfer a load to a part of the chassis where reinforcements lie, in which case multiple layers will be oriented so that their fibres run in that direction. Conversely, if multiple layers are oriented so that their fibres run in a *variety* of directions, loads will be dissipated over a wide area. The types of carbonfibre specified for each region, layer on layer, vary according to the nature of the loads which must be dealt with there.

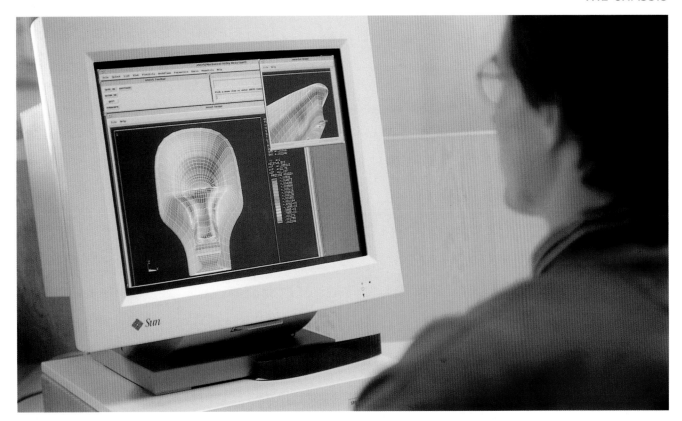

Given the complexity of both the chassis structure and the forces acting upon it, calculating the most effective way to build a strong, rigid, resilient yet lightweight structure would be nightmarishly difficult were it not for advanced computing power.

Of the many advanced computer-based techniques applied in the design and manufacture of Champ Cars, the key technique for structural measurements and calculations is Finite Element Analysis (FEA). Like carbonfibre, FEA found its way into race-car design from the aerospace industry. It is a computerised method of predicting and analysing the structural characteristics of key components at the design stage with a high degree of accuracy, and Champ Car designers and regulators employ it to help create components which are structurally highly efficient, yet also lightweight.

Although the structural characteristics of a component such as a chassis are infinitely complex, by breaking the structure down into a finite number of elements by computer, it becomes possible to analyse its behaviour under the influence of a wide variety of loads and calculate the most effective way to manufacture it.

Champ Car manufacturers employ specialist composites engineers within their design teams. Once an analysis is completed, the results can be displayed to them in graphical form, with values colour-coded to aid interpretation (as seen on-screen here, in an FEA representation of a Champ Car nosebox). In addition, the deformations (flexing) of a component can be represented in such a way that extremely small movements are artificially exaggerated on-screen, making it easier to identify the areas where movement is taking place.

Without the insights offered by FEA, a greater margin for error would have to be factored into the chassis construction, and the resulting structure would be heavier than necessary. Worse still, if the margin was insufficient, structural breakages would occur and the car would be downright dangerous. Identifying stress concentrations likely to result in structural failure – allowing designers and regulators to eliminate them – is a key FEA capability.

TECHNOLOGY OF THE CHAMP CAR

The first step in actually manufacturing the chassis panels is producing the patterns. This stage in the gestation of a car marks the transition from CAD (Computer-Aided Design) to CAM (Computer-Aided Manufacture), because the same computer software used to design the car now helps with the process of physically constructing it.

Although there are several different techniques for producing chassis panel patterns, and each manufacturer has its own preferred method, they all produce essentially the same results. The method described here is the most common, and begins when the appropriate data from the CAD system are fed into an automated routing machine, which fashions the patterns from either a proprietary pattern-making material – usually Cibatool – or from mahogany.

Cibatool is a Ciba Speciality Chemicals product which is delivered in slab form. Although it is a man-made material, it has similar properties to wood. However, it is easier to work than wood, being grainless, and it is virtually impervious to moisture-retention and thermal expansion, so patterns made from Cibatool retain their size and shape very precisely. As supplied, slabs of Cibatool are only 5 cm (2 in) thick, so the larger patterns must be made by stacking and gluing several slabs together.

The pattern-making material is secured firmly to a surface table beneath the router head to prevent any slippage while cutting takes place. The router head moves in swathes, back and forth, removing material with relentless precision until the required form is created.

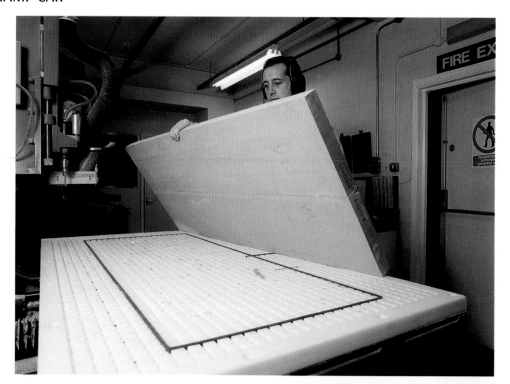

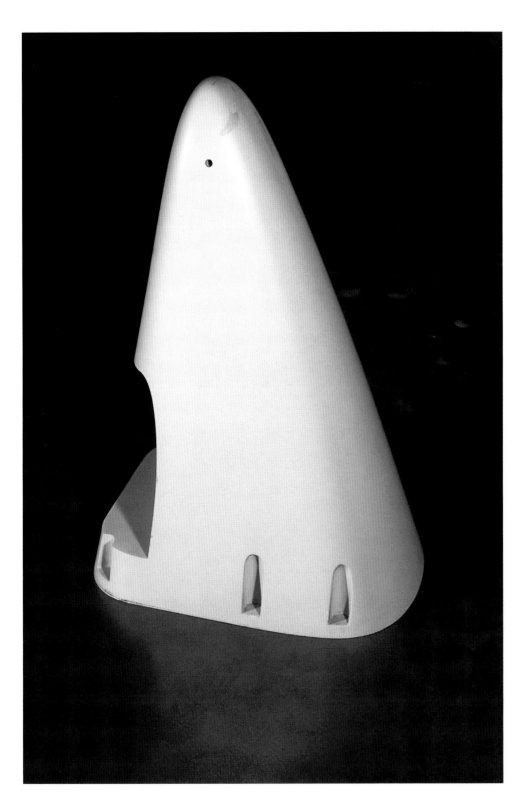

When all of the chassis patterns have been produced, they are bolted together temporarily so that their external surfaces can be sanded by hand with wet-or-dry paper. This process is called 'shaping through', and it ensures that the interfaces between adjoining patterns blend smoothly from one to the other. It also removes the faint machining marks left by the router – otherwise they would subsequently become imprinted on the moulds, and thus be transferred to the external surfaces of the completed chassis.

After 'shaping through', a coat of epoxy paint is applied to each of the chassis patterns to protect them from chemical attack by the resins in the carbonfibre when the moulds are laid up on them at the next stage of the process. The patterns are then ovened at a specified temperature to harden the paint – and stabilise it by releasing any volatile chemicals – then they are hand-sanded with very fine wet-or-dry paper and rubbed with T-Cut to produce a super-smooth surface finish.

Finally, the chassis patterns are temporarily bolted back together and fixed to a large surface table, so that a three-axis digitising machine can 'scan' the full pattern and confirm that its shape is faithful to the original CAD data.

When all this is done, the patterns are separated and sent to the mould-making department (the completed pattern for the nosebox is pictured here).

The moulds from which the chassis panels will be produced are made by laying up carbonfibre on the patterns to form a 'reflected' reproduction of what will be the end product. Carbonfibre is used for the moulds because it offers good resistance to the expansion and distortion which would otherwise occur when the moulds are exposed to the very high temperatures necessary to cure the panels.

Before any carbonfibre can be laid up, the patterns must be thoroughly prepared for mould-making. A ledge – known as a weir or return – is added to the outer perimeter of each pattern, so that the finished moulds will have a strengthening, stiffening angle around their edges when they are removed. Some of the moulds will be made in several pieces to aid removal of the completed panels – particularly in cases where a panel might otherwise become 'trapped' in its mould – so additional weirs are incorporated at the divisions.

To ensure that the finished moulds will separate cleanly, each pattern is given several coats of a release agent and buffed to a high sheen with several coats of hard wax.

Only then does mould-making begin: the procedures are similar to those employed when the chassis panels themselves are produced – described next – except that the moulds have very modest structural requirements, and therefore have only a single-skin construction with no aluminium honeycomb sandwich layer.

Pictured here is a nearly completed mould for the upper half of a chassis. Note the weirs which have been added around the outer edges of the pattern.

Before laying-up of the chassis panels can take place, the moulds must be thoroughly prepared. Each mould is degreased (usually with a solvent such as Acetone) to remove any contaminants, then receives as many as ten coats of a release agent. Each coat is left to evaporate before the next application, and the surface is buffed to maintain a high surface sheen. The mould is then ovened to harden the release agent, baking it into the surface.

This lengthy process is only necessary for the first use of each mould. For the production of subsequent panels, the moulds are given just a single coat of release agent.

The laying-up of composite materials within the moulds to form the chassis panels is a meticulous process in which highly skilled laminators closely follow the explicit written and diagrammatical instructions of the composites engineer, which are based on a combination of his earlier FEA work and his observance of the edicts of the regulatory body. The composites engineer stands in close attendance when the first example of each panel is being laid up, adjusting the precise manner in which the materials are assembled in the mould in a way that is only possible now that the job has departed the theoretical world of computational predictions and can at last be viewed in true 3D.

'Tweaking' the lay-up in this way is perfectly acceptable to the governing body, provided the alterations do not result in transgressions of CART's strict rulings on lay-up specifications.

While the process of producing the inner and outer carbonfibre skins of the chassis panels is essentially the same as that employed for the production of the moulds, the laying-up of the carbonfibre pieces in this case involves far more complex combinations of material types and fibre orientations – all painstakingly tailored to produce the exact structural properties required of each panel.

It is essential, when laying up the carbonfibre, that the material conforms to the contours of the mould and does not bridge any of the corners or other features, so the

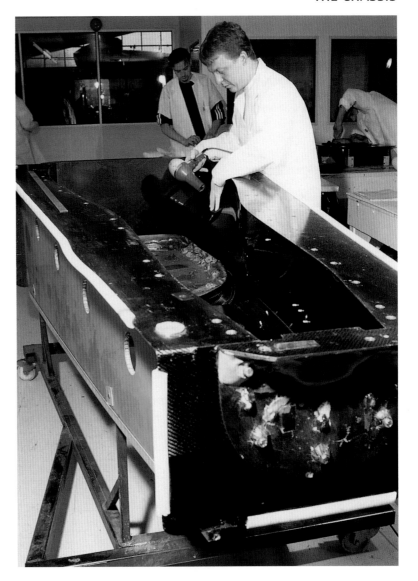

laminators warm it through with hair-dryers to soften the resin, making the fabric more pliable. The fact that the resin is already impregnated within the fibres simplifies the task of laying up the carbonfibre, as it makes the material slightly sticky at room temperature, preventing it from slipping from vertical surfaces after it has been pressed on. This quality is known as 'tack'.

In addition to hair-dryers, the laminators use surgical blades and spatulas to work the material into and around the features of the mould, taking care to ensure that pockets of air do not become trapped between plies. Adjoining pieces of carbonfibre are overlapped to create a thoroughly integrated structure. The carbonfibre pieces, as supplied to them, are slightly oversized so that the laminators can trim them down to create precisely the correct amount of overlap.

Pictured here is the first piece of carbonfibre being laid up in the mould for the upper half of a chassis (it is effectively upside down in this form).

After the first two or three layers of carbonfibre have been laid up, steps are taken to compact them together and force them against the contours of the mould to ensure a faithful reproduction of the intended form. This is achieved by enveloping the mould/panel combination in a carefully tailored vacuum bag and placing it in a large airtight chamber known as an autoclave, where it is subjected to a combination of a high vacuum state and a moderate temperature rise. This process is known as 'consolidation and debulking', and it is repeated several times as the layers of carbonfibre are built up.

As part of this process, there are various options for simultaneously drawing off the excess resin which 'bleeds out' of the carbonfibre. The precise amount of resin drawn off depends upon the fibre-to-resin ratio the composites engineer and the regulatory authority wish to achieve: this ratio has a critical bearing on the structural performance of the end product. A layer of cotton wool-like polyester cloth known as a breather layer is sandwiched between the outer layer of carbonfibre and the inner face of the vacuum bag, upon which excess resin and various volatile chemicals become deposited. A non-stick film known as a release layer, placed between the breather layer and the carbonfibre, ensures that the two do not stick together.

A rigid (aluminium or composite) plate – known variously as a pressure plate, a caul plate or an intensifier – can also be employed, again optionally, to bring more direct pressure down onto the carbonfibre layers.

When all of the carbonfibre layers which constitute a complete skin have been laid up in the mould, the mould/panel combination is enveloped in a vacuum bag once again and returned to the autoclave. This time, the vacuum state within the bag is augmented by much higher temperatures, and by extreme pressure (as high as 100 psi) from the autoclave – compressing the layers tight together to produce a super-strong structure.

A complete chassis skin is usually subjected to this treatment for around two-and-a-half hours, which cures it – turning it rock hard. The skin is only a few millimetres thick when completed.

Chassis panels are autoclaved three times during the manufacturing process: once after the first carbonfibre skin has been laid up, again after the aluminium honeycomb sandwich layer has been incorporated, and a third and final time after the second skin has been laid up.

TECHNOLOGY OF THE CHAMP CAR

The thickness of the layer of aluminium honeycomb sandwiched between the two carbonfibre skins varies considerably. Its thickness is dictated by the regulator and the composites engineer, based upon the varying structural demands on different regions of the chassis. The honeycomb is supplied to the laminators in pre-cut form and must be positioned with great precision, because if it does not adhere evenly to both skins, the structural loads will be unevenly distributed.

A sheet of neat resin is applied between the skins and the honeycomb layer, creating an exceptionally strong bond when cured.

At points where bolts and other types of fastener will pass through the chassis walls to retain components such as the engine and suspension mounts, the safety harness anchors and so forth, localised reinforcements known as inserts are set into the aluminium honeycomb layer. Without them, the bolts would move about under the forces acting upon them, crushing the honeycomb and fracturing the carbonfibre skins. The inserts are supplied to the laminator in pre-cut form, with holes already drilled through them, and are typically made from either solid aluminium or a very high-density resin-impregnated material tradenamed Tufnol.

After the honeycomb layer and inserts have been integrated with the first skin in the autoclave, the second skin is laid up on top. The mould/panel combination is then returned to the autoclave for the final curing cycle, after which the panel is prised from its mould.

The carbonfibre/aluminium honeycomb sandwich construction is pictured in cross-section here.

On completion of the moulding process, panels are sent for 'finishing' and assembly into a complete chassis structure. Two chassis panels have to be removable: the nosebox and the damper cover (the latter is situated immediately in

front of the cockpit aperture and will cover the inboard elements of the front suspension). The nosebox is produced in exactly the same manner as the other chassis panels, with two skins of carbonfibre sandwiching a layer of aluminium honeycomb. The damper cover is produced in a slightly different way: because it is not a load-bearing component, it has a single-skin construction with no honeycomb layer.

The quantity of chassis panels produced varies according to the anticipated attrition rate for each panel type. Needless to say, noseboxes tend to be produced in the largest quantities!

Before the upper and lower halves of the chassis are joined together – by a combination of rivets and epoxy resin around a circumferential tongue-in-groove joint – the three internal bulkheads are bonded in with epoxy adhesive. One is the master cylinder bulkhead, which is the subject of a more detailed description in the next chapter. The second is the dash bulkhead: a flat 'hoop' through which the driver's legs pass, located just forward of the cockpit aperture so as to serve as a forward rollover bar. The third is the seat-back: a sculpted panel located directly behind the driver's seat, so as to form a partition between the fuel cell compartment and the cockpit.

All three bulkheads have essentially the same carbonfibre/aluminium honeycomb sandwich construction as the rest of the chassis, and their presence contributes to the overall strength and rigidity of the structure by providing internal reinforcement and countering any tendency it might have to lozenge under cornering or impact loads.

'Finishing' of chassis panels primarily involves enlarging, and/or tapping and/or countersinking the holes in the various inserts where all of the internal and external components will be mounted later (access to awkward areas is easier while the chassis is still in pieces). Some manufacturers have sophisticated five-axis automated drilling machines to undertake this task, but others prefer to do it manually using a system of templates. Either way, the chassis panels are anchored squarely to steel jigs to ensure a high standard of accuracy.

Typical examples of the locations of these holes are: on the upper half of the chassis, at the points where the inboard elements of the front suspension will be mounted; at the front of the chassis, for the nosebox attachments; on the sides of the chassis, for the side-pod attachments; at the rear of the chassis, for the engine mounts; and on the bottom of the chassis, where the aerodynamic underbody will be mounted.

CART regulations specify that a firewall must be fitted at some point between the engine compartment and the cockpit. This must either be made of metal at least 1.587 mm (0.0625 in) thick, or another fire-retardant material approved by CART. It is usually machined from a solid plate of aluminium by an automated CAD/CAM process, as pictured here, and serves as the rear face of the chassis. The large aperture at the centre of the firewall is to allow access to the fuel cell internals.

chapter 2 CRASHWORTHINESS

CHAMP Cars are stronger and sturdier than their Formula 1 brethren. Massive impact forces result from high-speed collisions with the concrete walls which adjoin many of the racetracks, and because the tyre walls, guardrails and run-off areas mandated for Formula 1 are not feasible at these circuits, the cars must be more robust to compensate.

As in Formula 1, it is a mandatory requirement for Champ Cars to carry an aircraft-style 'black box' to record vital information which would help investigators to identify the cause of a serious accident. Impact forces of up to 100 G have been recorded in some accidents.

evolving in response to accidents and incidents as they arise. For example, in 1992 there was a series of crashes in which drivers sustained serious leg injuries when noseboxes were broken off in the initial impact with the wall, then the fronts of the chassis were shattered by secondary impacts. In response, CART mandated the introduction of a new internal bulkhead situated a minimum of 305 mm (12 in) aft of the front face of the chassis – effectively creating an extension to the front of the chassis, so that even with the nosebox detached there is a sufficient amount of deformable structure in front of the drivers' feet and legs to prevent serious injury.

The ruling also called for this new internal bulkhead to carry the master cylinders, thereby reducing the risk of these being driven through the front face of the chassis and into the footwell in a major frontal impact.

There are other examples. To prevent drivers being injured by components such as suspension arms penetrating the cockpit wall in heavy impacts, CART regulations require a 30-thou layer of 'anti-ballistic' material to be incorporated within the lay-up in specified regions of the chassis.

TECHNOLOGY OF THE CHAMP CAR

CART's mandatory crash-tests are just as stringent as those required for Formula 1, but there are fewer of them. In the United Kingdom, where the vast majority of Champ Cars are manufactured, CART-mandated crash testing is undertaken at the Cranfield Impact Centre, part of the Cranfield Institute of Technology near Bedford. The crash-test facilities there – which are also used by virtually all of the Formula 1 teams – can be hired for around £2500 a day, complete with expert personnel.

A compulsory frontal impact test simulates a head-on collision, and is designed to assess the ability of the chassis structure in general – and the nosebox in particular – to dissipate the kinetic energy which is released at the moment of impact, so that the driver is saved from injurious deceleration forces. CART regulations for the frontal impact test stipulate that there should be an initial and then a secondary impact, recognising that this is the most probable scenario in a real accident.

When the frontal impact test is undertaken at Cranfield Impact Centre, the test criteria are met by fixing a sample section of the forward chassis structure – with nosebox attached – to a steel plate 25 mm (1 in) thick, and striking it with a mass of 900 kg (1984.5 lb). The steel plate is immovable, being set in a huge concrete block, and the impacting mass – a ballasted sled – produces a representative impact energy.

The sled is propelled by a system of bungee cords down a 15-metre (50-ft) ramp inclined at an angle of 11 degrees, impacting the forward chassis/nosebox structure twice in succession with a specified force. The sled is hauled backwards by a length of chain to the top of the ramp, where it is held by steel jaws. When it is released, it literally *flies* down the ramp, because it is borne on four air-bearings instead of wheels to ensure virtually frictionless movement (this guarantees consistency from one run to another). The first impact generates a force of 58.5 KJ, with an impact speed of 11.4 metres per second (37.43 feet per second) – 41.27 kph (25.65 mph). The second impact generates a force of 29.25 KJ, with an impact speed of 8.06 metres per second (26.44 feet per second) – 29.19 kph (18.14 mph).

Such speeds may seem unrepresentative of an actual Champ Car collision, but bear in mind that the impacting mass strikes the nosebox head-on, with no deflection – and that the steel plate the chassis section is fixed to, and the impacting mass itself, yield *not an inch*.

CART regulations stipulate that, in both impacts, the average deceleration of the sled must not exceed 40 G. The peak deceleration may be as high as 80 G, but only for a maximum of 10 milliseconds. Two accelerometers mounted on the sled measure its deceleration at the moment of impact, while the impact speed is measured by photo-electric cells. Data from either accelerometer is sufficient to support the test, for each acts as a back-up to the other should one fail at the crucial moment.

If the composites engineer has done his job properly, the nosebox should collapse progressively, absorbing most of the impact energy. Damage to the chassis itself must not extend any further back than the master cylinder bulkhead.

To aid subsequent analysis, the impact sequence can be recorded by a high-speed camera running at, typically, 2000 frames per second.

A 'nose push-off test' simulates an accident in which the nosebox is struck heavily from the side. The intention is to verify that the nosebox will not become detached from the chassis in these circumstances, denuding the car of its most vital energy-absorbing structure. The front aerofoils are strong enough to act as levers in this type of impact, wrenching the nosebox off.

Unlike the frontal impact simulation described earlier, the nose push-off test is a static – as opposed to dynamic – test: that is to say, impact forces are simulated by steady pressure, rather than actually being delivered by one object forcibly striking another.

In preparation for the test, a sample section of the forward chassis structure, with nosebox attached, is anchored firmly to a sturdy tubular-steel framework. An oblong steel plate measuring 30 x 10 cm (12 x 4 in) is positioned against the side of the chassis, as close as possible to the interface with the nosebox, bracing the chassis firmly against the substantial loadings that are about to be exerted from the opposite side.

A second plate of identical dimensions is then positioned on the opposite side, on the nosebox itself, mid-way between its mountings and its foremost extremity. Unlike the other plate, which is fixed in position, this plate can translate slowly in a lateral direction by means of a worm-drive mechanism, exerting loadings equivalent to a major sideways impact. The worm drive is equipped with a load cell to measure the lateral forces exerted on the nosebox.

The plate is driven slowly into the side of the nosebox until a force of 30 kN (3 tons) has been exerted, and then held for 30 seconds before being slowly eased away. If this cycle is performed without any evidence of structural failure – either cracking of the nosebox or damage to its mounting points – the chassis is deemed to have passed this test.

Two crash-test simulations are conducted on the areas of the chassis adjacent to the cockpit. In both cases, only a small section of the structure is presented for testing. The first is a dynamic side-impact simulation, in which successive specimens of a section of the cockpit wall measuring no less than 260 mm (10 in) in length by 104 mm (4 in) in depth are struck with increasing force by an impacting mass measuring 26 mm (1 in) in diameter until damage or deformation becomes visible on the inner skin. For each successive test, measurements of the impact forces, and measurements and photographs of both sides of the impact area, must be submitted to CART for analysis.

The second is a static test and concentrates on a section of the rim around the top of the cockpit aperture measuring 382 mm (15 in) long by at least 76 mm (3 in) deep. A steel plate measuring 26 mm (1 in) in diameter is slowly driven down onto the centre of this specimen until it fractures. Again, detailed measurements and photographs documenting the test are submitted for CART's inspection.

Rear-impact crashes can be spectacular – as evidenced by Nigel Mansell's famous accident at Phoenix International Raceway in 1993, pictured here. Unlike Formula 1 cars, Champ Cars are not required to carry a rear-impact absorption structure on the aft end of the gearbox. However, the design and construction of the cars – as dictated by the regulations – reflect the importance CART attaches to providing adequate rear-impact protection for the drivers. The driver's headrest and seat are the subject of particular attention: high-energy-absorbing padding must be incorporated into the areas most likely to come into contact with the driver's head, and there are regulations governing the thickness of the seat material.

To verify the performance of the cockpit padding material, there is a CART-mandated dynamic test in which a mass representing a driver's helmeted head – it weighs 6 kg (13.23 lb) and has a diameter of 254 mm (10 in) – strikes the same area of the padding at a perpendicular angle twice in succession. The speed of the initial impact is 6.7 metres per second (21.98 feet per second), while the speed of the secondary impact is 4.5 metres per second (14.76 feet per second). The test is conducted twice – at 25 and 38 degrees C – because the energy-absorption properties of the padding alter as a function of temperature.

Deceleration of the impacting mass must not exceed a peak value of 150 G for this test to be deemed successful.

Champ Cars must be designed and constructed to provide maximum protection to the driver in the event of a rollover accident – as in this case, when Michael Andretti's Swift went spectacularly out of control at Mid-Ohio. The most visible evidence of this protection is the rollover hoop, situated immediately above the driver's head. Although this structure is integral with the rest of the chassis, having two multi-ply carbonfibre skins sandwiching an aluminium honeycomb layer, at its centre is a hoop of SAE 4130 or BSI T45 seamless steel alloy tubing a minimum of 34.925 mm (1.375 in) in diameter and with a minimum wall thickness of 2.41 mm (0.095 in), braced fore and aft with tubing of an identical standard, but a minimum of 26 mm (1 in) in diameter and with a minimum wall thickness of 2.03 mm (0.080 in).

The rollover hoop is also designed to facilitate lifting and towing of the race car.

chapter 3 AERODYNAMICS

AERODYNAMICS are the single most important factor in Champ Car design – probably accounting for as much as 80 per cent of the car's total performance. For hauling down the straightaways quicker than the next man, aerodynamic efficiency is obviously essential. But cornering is an even more important part of the aerodynamic equation, because a driver with a speed advantage on the exit to a corner will – all things being equal – maintain that advantage for the entire length of the following straight.

The aerodynamic devices, working in concert with the tyres, endow the modern Champ Car with phenomenal cornering ability. Lateral forces of up to 4.5 G can be generated through high-speed corners. By comparison, an ordinary roadgoing car cannot sustain a lateral force of much more than 1 G, because at about that point it loses its grip and starts to slide away.

Downforce is the key to this exceptional cornering performance: the creation of 'negative lift' – with aerodynamic devices performing the opposite function to the wings of an aircraft – pressing the car down onto the racetrack surface. This increases the grip of the tyres, allowing increased cornering speeds and aiding braking performance.

Most of a Champ Car's aerodynamic aids are composed of two skins of carbonfibre sandwiching a layer of aluminium honeycomb. They are produced by essentially the same process of pattern-making, mould-making and laying-up as was described for the manufacture of the chassis in Chapter 1.

A Champ Car is, in essence, a 'dirty' shape aerodynamically – because CART regulations call for the cars to have open bodywork, with the wheels exposed rather than faired in – so the challenge of achieving high levels of aerodynamic efficiency is a considerable one.

Although the racetrack is the ultimate proving ground, the windtunnel is where this challenge is met.

An exquisitely detailed scale model is created for windtunnel testing – one in which every relevant feature of the full-sized car is faithfully reproduced. Most of the windtunnels employed for Champ Car testing accommodate 40- to 50-per cent scale models. During the course of testing, dozens of 'bolt-on' modifications are tried to see if they improve performance: alternatively shaped noseboxes, underbody profiles and sidepod air intakes, different combinations of front and rear aerofoils, and so forth. Aerodynamic effects in different regions of the car tend to be interrelated, so the process is a complex one. Aerodynamicists are also aware that external factors will influence the performance of their car: a gust of wind, or turbulent air from the car in front.

Windtunnel testing is not limited to the gestation period of a new car – although that is certainly when the workload is most concentrated. It continues during the course of the season, as refinements are developed in the endless quest for better performance.

There is much more to a windtunnel than first meets the eye. Published photographs of windtunnels in operation usually show the windtunnel model suspended from a streamlined strut in the area known as the working section, but that is but one small part of the overall facility. Out of sight, a huge fan impels the flow of air which passes over the model. The air travels a considerable distance to reach the working section. It is accelerated just before it gets there by the walls, floor and ceiling converging to form what is termed a contraction nozzle.

In most of the windtunnels used for Champ Car testing, after exiting the working section, the airflow is recirculated back through the fan to pass over the model time after time. This helps to ensure consistent test results, because if fresh air is drawn in from outside it can introduce temperature fluctuations into the windtunnel airstream, altering the air density unpredictably.

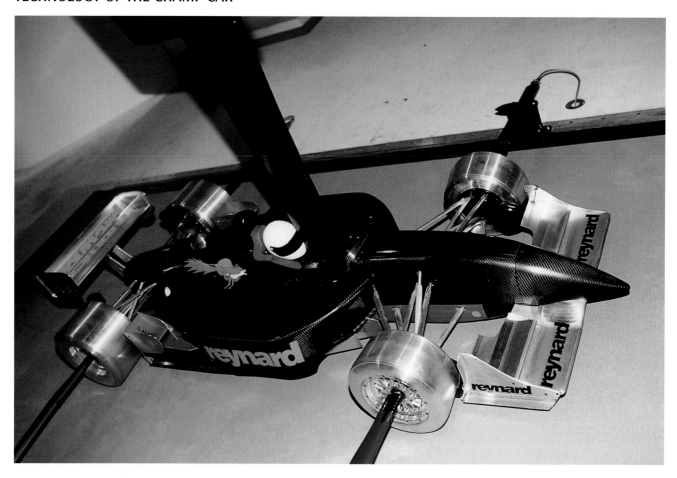

To recreate actual conditions as accurately as possible, the windtunnel model is suspended above a moving belt which simulates the relative movement of the racetrack surface beneath the car's wheels. The 'moving ground', as it is called, is akin to a conveyor belt and moves at a speed which corresponds with the speed of the airflow passing through the windtunnel – again, to accurately simulate actual conditions.

Sometimes, the four wheel/tyre assemblies are not actually fixed to the windtunnel model. Instead, they are positioned a fractional distance away from it – individually supported on horizontal struts mounted on either side of the moving belt – and they rest on the belt, which rotates them at a proportionate speed. This arrangement (pictured here) allows the drag levels on each wheel/tyre unit to be independently measured by load cells installed in each strut.

Due to their large size – and uncompromising shape! – the tyres create appreciable drag: around one-third of the car's total drag in road-circuit and street-circuit trim, rising to as much as half of the car's total drag in Superspeedway trim. Race car aerodynamicists wish to assess how tyre drag levels are influenced by changes made to other parts of the car.

The streamlined strut from which the model is suspended is part of a complex system which measures the major aerodynamic forces acting on the model. The resulting data are fed to a computer in the windtunnel control room, overlooking the working section. Aerodynamicists place particular emphasis on three parameters: downforce, drag and balance.

Downforce levels should be increased during the course of a sustained windtunnel testing programme as a result of modifications made to the model through constant experimentation. It is necessary to have an elaborate suction system immediately beneath the working section to keep the moving belt uniformly flat, because – despite its modest size – the model racing car generates considerable downforce and would otherwise draw parts of the belt up towards it.

Drag levels play a critical part in aerodynamic performance, because drag not only impairs the car's speed potential, but also degrades its fuel economy. Aerodynamicists attempt to increase downforce whilst not increasing drag.

Balance, as the term applies to racing car aerodynamics, means optimising the contributions of the front and rear aerofoils to bring the car's downforce levels, front to rear, into equilibrium. The term could also be applied to the car's sensitivity to changes in pitch and heave. Changes in pitch occur when the car pitches nose-up under acceleration or nose-down under braking; these cause the car's centre of pressure to shift fore and aft, which destabilises it. Key objectives of windtunnel testing are to both minimise this centre-of-pressure shift and improve the car's tolerance to shifts when they occur. Changes in heave are vertical translations (changes in ride-height) as the car passes over undulations in the racetrack surface; these also destabilise the car, because they cause its downforce levels to vary unpredictably. Computer-controlled servos can alter the model's pitch angle and ride-height remotely while the windtunnel is in operation, allowing aerodynamicists to assess the effects such movements have on the car's balance.

Swift is unique among Champ Car manufacturers in having the luxury of its own windtunnel – at its San Clemente, California headquarters – although, in common with the other Champ Car manufacturers, it does not test constantly, so it offers windtunnel time to other users on a commercial basis through its Swift Aero subsidiary.

Reynard hires a windtunnel operated by the UK Ministry of Defence's Royal Military College of Science at Shrivenham, near Swindon – although it is building a windtunnel at its Indianapolis facility for use by its customers. Penske hires the windtunnel facilities at the University of Southampton on England's south coast – not far from Poole, where its cars are designed and built. Lola currently hires the windtunnel at the Cranfield Institute of Technology – the same place where the British-based Champ Car manufacturers undertake their crash testing.

The amount of windtunnel testing a manufacturer undertakes varies according to whether it has its own windtunnel, or has to share testing time with the windtunnel owner or other users of a proprietary windtunnel, in which case availability, workload and budgetary limitations can come into play. Penske, as an example, tests on a one-week-in/two-weeks-away basis throughout the year.

It is ironic that America's flagship single-seat racing category is dominated by British-built cars, but the tide may be beginning to turn. Launched into Champ Car racing with finance from Hiro Matsushita – a former driver and scion of the Panasonic dynasty – Swift Engineering is a relative newcomer to CART's ranks – but it has made a significant impact. In 1997, a Swift made history by becoming the first US-made car in 14 years to win a Champ Car race.

A healthy bank balance has allowed Swift to invest heavily in technological infrastructure. The impressive windtunnel at San Clemente is a shining example: it has even been used by some of the Formula 1 teams, most notably Williams and Stewart.

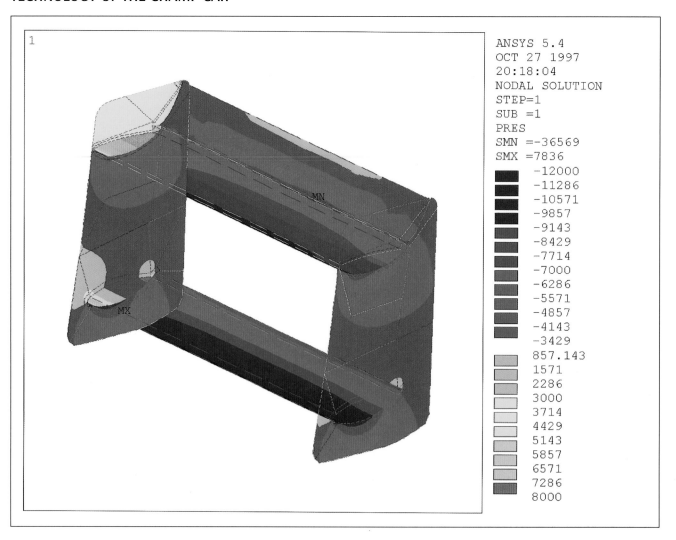

Continuing advances in technology are altering the nature of aerodynamic testing. In the windtunnel, laser beams are now being used to 'visualise' turbulence and to measure the airflow at specific points. Lasers offer the benefit of being able to accurately measure the characteristics of the airflow without physically interfering with it.

Also, windtunnel testing is being increasingly complemented by computer-based analysis of airflow behaviour. A technique known as Computational Fluid Dynamics (CFD) allows the aerodynamic performance of particular shapes to be predicted before a windtunnel model is actually built. CFD also allows comparisons to be made with the results of physically testing models in the windtunnel, in order to increase the accuracy of testing techniques.

As with the FEA structural analysis technique described in Chapter 1, the results of CFD analyses can be presented in a colour-coded form which simplifies interpretation. Champ Car manufacturers are understandably protective of their FEA imagery. To illustrate the general principle, the FEA image above shows the air pressure distribution on the rear aerofoil assembly of a Formula 3 car.

A Champ Car's most important aerodynamic device is usually invisible to the spectator, but is pictured here during the production process. It is the underbody: a panel of carbonfibre/aluminium honeycomb sandwich construction, comprising three surfaces – a central 'keel' with an elevated surface on either side – attached directly to the underside of the chassis.

The underbody acts in concert with the system of tunnels at its aft extremity. The relationship between the underbody and these tunnels is one of interdependence. The tunnels have an upward-sloping shape which widens the gap between the undersurface of the car and the racetrack surface, causing the airflow there to slow down in the same way that the flow of water slows down when a river becomes wider. When an airflow slows down its pressure increases, causing the air to be expelled more rapidly from the back of the tunnels. This, in turn, draws air from beneath the underbody, accelerating it, and as that air accelerates its pressure decreases – creating downforce which sucks the car onto the racetrack surface.

The underbody has a 'stepped' configuration by order of the regulations, to limit its efficiency. A flat underbody would produce even more downforce, increasing lap speeds to unacceptable levels. The 'steps' on the underbody are 50.8 mm (2 in) deep.

Unlike their Formula 1 brethren, Champ Cars are still 'ground effect' cars. Because CART regulations allow a comparatively broad scope of freedom in the design of the underbody tunnels, Champ Cars are far more sophisticated from the aerodynamic standpoint than their Grand Prix counterparts.

The tunnels start about half-way along the underbody, roughly below the point where the engine meets the chassis. Sculpted around the engine and gearbox, and also running beneath the aft sections of the sidepods, they extend back into the space between the rear wheels. There is one large central tunnel and two smaller tunnels, one on either side. The wording of the regulations also allows what are classed as 'features' – but which are actually miniature tunnels – to be incorporated alongside them. Provided they do not rise above the plane of the bottom surface of the underbody by more than 76.2 mm (3 in), these 'features' are not officially classed as tunnels.

The shapes and positions of the tunnels and 'features' are determined by relentless windtunnel testing. There are an almost infinite number of permutations in tunnel shape. Variables include the 'break point' – the point where a tunnel departs from the flat plane of the underbody – the tunnel entry width, the roof profile, the wall profile, and the engine and gearbox shapes. Changes to any and all of these parameters have an effect, and all interact with the other parameters and with the aerodynamic characteristics of the rest of the car.

During the windtunnel testing programme for its 1998-model car, Penske assessed 20 different roof profiles – and as many wall profiles – in order to find the most efficient combination. Such testing is an evolutionary process. It would be too time-consuming to make a new underbody/tunnel model for every permutation, so the modelmakers produce a 'host' underbody which can accommodate interchangeable pieces, built up like a jigsaw puzzle. When a final shape is decided upon, a definitive underbody/tunnel model is made.

Aerodynamicists aim to achieve the optimum – as opposed to the maximum – level of downforce, because they have constant regard for the aerodynamic balance of the car, seeking to engender stability by alleviating the unsettling effects of braking, accelerating and negotiating undulations in the racetrack surface.

The maximum permissible tunnel depth and width have been reduced over the years, restricting the volume of air passing through them in order to reduce downforce. In 1996, CART introduced a significant reduction in tunnel depth, from 203.2 mm (8 in) down to 152.4 mm (6 in). This ruling applies only to the tunnel *exit*: the tunnel itself can be any depth relative to the plane of the bottom surface of the underbody, provided it comes back down to 152.4 mm (6 in) at the exit.

The entry of air to the underbody is the key factor governing what happens to the airflow passing through the tunnels. The regulations allow the forward part of the underbody to incorporate some profiling to aid this flow. Aerodynamicists must promote the most efficient possible flow of air into the tunnels, and they do so in a very novel way – by producing vortices. A vortex, rich with negative pressure, is a far more potent source of aerodynamic energy than a purely uniform airflow, because the swirling effect within the vortex accelerates the air and gives it more 'zest'. This energy is harnessed and channelled to maximum effect.

The key is to position the vortices in the right places, so they will energise the airflow at critical points. That is achieved by extensive experimentation with devices called vortex generators - small vertical plates incorporating subtle curves - positioned on either side of the car, low down, just ahead of the sidepods. Vortex generators are a very highly evolved, and secret, feature of the modern Champ Car. The flow of air over and away from them is extremely complex.

Vortex generation is something of a black art, and Champ Car designers are loath to talk about it for fear of conceding a hard-earned advantage. There are probably two main vortices tripped by each generator - one off the leading edge, and one off the trailing edge - and then there is probably a 'sheet vortex' produced as well. Understanding the complex interplay between these vortices and the rest of the car in the windtunnel, trying to assess which vortex is doing what, is a very demanding exercise.

Of particular difficulty is understanding where a vortex goes once it has been shed, and getting it back in the right place on the underbody - because some vortices actually arc away from the car and then swoop back under it. Race car aerodynamicists can employ a technique called flow visualisation in the windtunnel to physically 'see' what the airflow is doing. To visualise the *on-surface* airflow behaviour, streams of a non-setting white paint (a paraffin-based emulsion) are flowed over the model. When the test is over, the paint patterns leave an accurate trace of the airflow's characteristics. To visualise *off-surface* airflow behaviour, a stream of white smoke is passed over the model from a hand-held metal 'wand'.

Different sizes, shapes and combinations of vortex generators are fitted according to the aerodynamic requirements of particular cars at particular circuits, and their design constantly evolves.

Aerodynamically, a Champ Car in road or street circuit configuration is very different from a car in Superspeedway trim. This is partially due to the regulations – which prescribe different aerodynamic specifications for different types of circuit – and partially due to the very different nature of the aerodynamic demands on the car. On oval circuits, the banking allows the cars to negotiate corners much faster, while the ensuing higher speeds make slipstreaming down the straights a key element of the driver's craft.

The front aerofoil assembly usually has two aerofoil elements on either side for races on road, street and one-mile oval circuits, but CART regulations permit only a single element for races on the larger ovals, including Superspeedways, in order to reduce downforce. On the larger ovals and the Superspeedways there is a smaller front aerofoil allowance in any case, reducing downforce still further: the maximum permissible length is reduced from 160 cm (63 in) to 142.24 cm (56 in) and the maximum permissible chord (the distance between the leading edge and the trailing edge) is 203 mm (8 in).

Within the scope defined by the regulations, the clearance between the front aerofoil assembly and the racetrack surface can be adjusted, as can the aerofoil angle or angles. The greater the angle, the greater the downforce generated. To increase downforce still further, a Gurney-flap can be fitted to the trailing edges of aerofoils. Named after the legendary American racing driver Dan Gurney – now a Champ Car team owner – the Gurney, or 'wicker', is a thin strip of carbonfibre which adds a small lip to the aerofoil shape, effectively increasing its curvature and thereby increasing the downforce it generates.

At the extremities of the front aerofoils are the endplates. These channel the airflow for maximum efficiency, by preventing it from 'spilling out' over the ends of the aerofoil elements and diminishing their effectiveness. They also help to smooth the flow of air around the front tyres, and often incorporate sculpted features to increase their effectiveness.

Although the front aerofoil assemblies provide substantial levels of downforce, the designer's primary purpose for them is to use that downforce to balance (trim) the car and to deliver a good quality of airflow to the underbody. When a car is closely following another, it can lose as much as 30 per cent of the downforce from its front aerofoils, because the turbulence created by the car in front diminishes their aerodynamic efficiency. This can be particularly treacherous on banked corners, because the destabilised car can easily drift wide onto the dirty part of the racetrack and hit the concrete retaining wall.

In Formula 1 in 1997, Ferrari introduced a front aerofoil constructed with a special carbonfibre lay-up which caused it to flex downwards at the ends under the influence of aerodynamic loads. In doing so, it closed the gap between the endplates and the racetrack surface, increasing its efficiency without creating more drag.

All structures flex to some extent under load, whether it is the wing of an aircraft or the shaft of a tennis racket. If they were too stiff they would break. Ferrari's innovative front aerofoil, with a pronounced flexing capability deliberately designed in, certainly posed problems for Formula 1's legislators – but this situation could not occur in Champ Car racing, because CART officials hang weights from specified areas of bodywork, including the aerofoils, and then take measurements to ensure that flexing has not exceeded certain prescribed limits.

This has now been acknowledged as the best way to prevent transgressions, because Formula 1's sanctioning body – the FIA – adopted it in 1998!

The positioning of the front aerofoils has a crucial influence on the characteristics of the airflow to the underbody. Different underbody designs react in different ways to alternative front aerofoil configurations. For example, some underbodies perform better if the front aerofoils are as low and as flat as possible, while others respond more favourably if as much of the front aerofoil area as possible is moved out of its path – hence the downswept (anhedral) front aerofoil assemblies seen on some cars.

Although the underbody is the main contributor to aerodynamic performance – especially when a car is in Superspeedway configuration, because the front and rear wings are emasculated by the regulations and produce relatively little downforce – the front aerofoil assembly's contribution is vital. It must do everything possible, however small, to help the underbody gain downforce.

The sidepods house the radiator ducts and 'fill' much of the space between the front and rear wheels with a streamlined structure. The airflow, having passed over the front tyres, must transit the upper surfaces of the side-pods before passing over the rear tyres and rear aerofoil assembly. The sidepod height has a bearing on the manner in which the airflow changes direction over those three regions, which in turn has a bearing on the total downforce generated by the car, and on its aerodynamic stability.

In fact, the length, height and shape of the sidepods have a bearing on the total lift-to-drag ratio of the car – which is a critical factor.

As well as carrying the airflow over the car, and producing a certain amount of downforce, the sidepods can also play an important role in reducing the overall drag of the car. By sloping and waisting them to the rear, de-signers can make significant aerodynamic performance gains.

Penske certainly took this principle to new levels with its 1998-model car (pictured right), which had a very small, very narrow transmission – allowing design chief John Travis to achieve a pronounced waisting effect which distinguished this car from the others. The way that the sidepods and engine cover tapered towards the rear of the car brought the Penske about as close as it is possible to get within the existing regulations to the classic 'teardrop' shape beloved by aerodynamicists.

The drag reduction resulting from this shape is probably due to the fact that the airflow remains attached to the surface of the car, rather than breaking away from it and becoming turbulent. To achieve such a shape within the confines of the regulations required fastidious attention to detail. All of the mechanical components at the rear of the Penske were very tightly packed together.

The position of the sidepod air intakes is clearly visible in this picture. The shape of these intakes is vitally important, and is determined by windtunnel testing. It is necessary to achieve the smoothest possible flow of air into the intakes, or the radiators will not be able to perform efficiently.

Over the years, the size of the sidepods has steadily increased. Designers used to try to keep the sidepods as small and as low as possible, but now they make them as big as they can within the limitations imposed by the regulations. They discovered that anything contained within the total frontal area of the car – as defined by the 'box' created by the wheels – made no appreciable difference to the overall drag level, so they may as well fill that area with sidepod volume and then make the most of them aerodynamically.

Large sidepods also make a welcome contribution to side-impact protection for the driver.

Housed within the sidepods are the carbonfibre radiator ducts. Their shape – which is determined by windtunnel testing – must be such that the airflow remains smooth on its journey to the radiators. If it becomes turbulent, there will not be an even distribution of cooling air across the full face of each radiator core and the engine will have a tendency to overheat.

Oversizing the radiators to compensate for any deficiencies in the radiator duct design is an unacceptable compromise, because additional radiator area incurs additional aerodynamic drag, as well as excess weight.

Lengths of Bowden cable passing through the radiator ducts are testimony to the huge downforce levels generated by the underbody. They anchor the underbody to the sides of the chassis – preventing its outer edges from being bent downwards by the force of the low-pressure zone beneath the car.

Air flowing out of the sidepods is of such a low velocity that it is of virtually no further use aerodynamically. By the time it has passed through the radiator cores, almost all of its energy has been dissipated: air entering a radiator at 310 kph (130 mph) typically exits it at less than 30 kph (20 mph).

To suit race conditions, teams can control the volume of air flowing through the radiators by either covering or exposing a series of vents in the sidepod flanks with removable hatches.

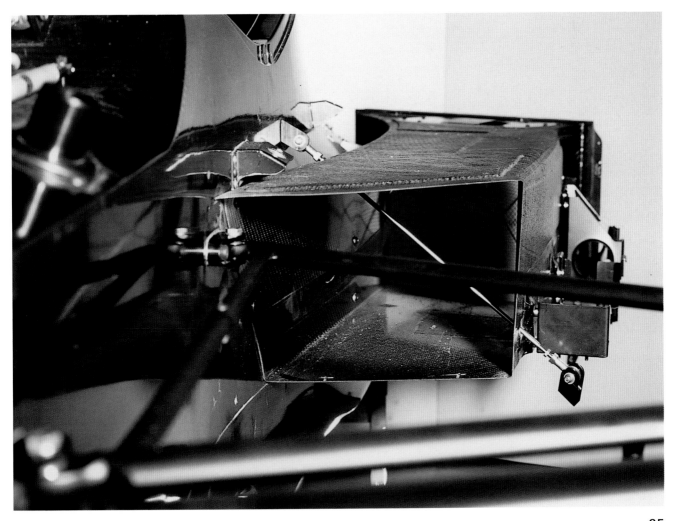

Reducing the levels of turbulence around the driver's helmet has become a priority in recent years, not only because turbulence can diminish the overall aerodynamic efficiency of the car, but also because it can upset a driver's concentration.

'Trip strips' and other sculpted features on the helmet – all perfected in the windtunnel – can reduce its tendency to lift at high speeds, and smooth out the airflow around the helmet to reduce buffeting. Some cars have a vestigial Perspex windscreen or a low-line carbonfibre fairing around the front of the cockpit opening for the same purpose.

Creating a recess for the driver's helmet at the base of the rollover hoop allows it to become an integral part of the car's shape. With the phenomenal speeds reached on some circuits – bearing in mind that aerodynamic drag increases as the square of the speed (doubling the speed increases the drag *four-fold*) – such obsessive attention to detail is not misplaced.

Although it has a very functional purpose – which is to house the engine, transmission and rear suspension – the engine cover also serves a key aerodynamic role. It must be as streamlined as possible, in order to allow the airflow to pass smoothly to the rear aerofoil assembly. And it must also have the minimum frontal area in order to reduce drag.

The engine cover hugs the contours of the highest and widest points on the engine and the gearbox-mounted suspension elements, terminating at the base of the mounting for the rear aerofoil assembly. At the sides, it flares out gracefully to meet the sidepods.

Many cars sport a shallow vertical fin on top of the engine cover – as seen on this Penske. This helps to control the flow of air to the rear aerofoil assembly.

Penske has had to weather an extended drought of race wins, with the competitiveness it once enjoyed dulled by the sheer strength of the Reynard onslaught. While Penske latterly has lacked pace, it simply oozes professionalism. Its standards of preparation are second to none, but for Roger Penske – a man accustomed to success – this is scant consolation. In engine supplier Mercedes-Benz, Penske has perhaps the ultimate technical partner. Mercedes' latest offering is a masterpiece of engineering innovation and attention to detail, yet the overall package has failed to fulfil expectations.

An historic 100th Champ Car win remained elusive for Penske as this book went to press.

The airflow around the rear tyres must be carefully controlled if the car is to be aerodynamically efficient. At the rear of the car, the sides curve inwards Coke bottle-style to control the airflow around the inner surfaces of the rear tyres and thereby reduce drag. Among the many factors which must be considered when refining the aerodynamics in this region is ensuring that the hot exhaust gases will not damage elements of the rear suspension.

Many cars have winglets mounted at the rear of the sidepods, immediately in front of the rear tyres, to generate extra downforce. In their place, some have graceful extensions of the upper-rear sections of the sidepods which generate additional downforce and assist the airflow's passage over the rear tyres. These are known variously as 'flip-ups', 'flugelhorns' or simply tyre deflectors.

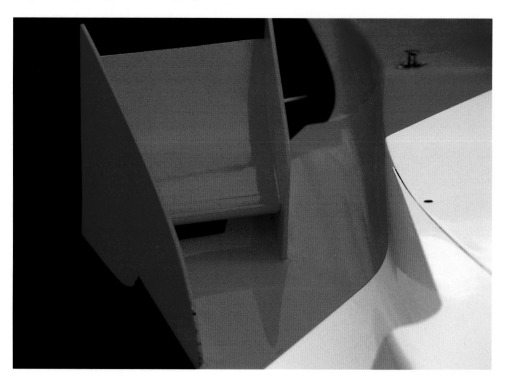

The rear aerofoil assembly is capable of generating up to one-third of the car's total downforce. Only a single horizontal rear aerofoil element is permitted for races on the larger ovals and the Superspeedways. A maximum of two elements may be fitted for the other types of circuit. As with the front aerofoil assembly, the clearance between the rear aerofoil assembly and the racetrack surface can be adjusted within the scope defined by the regulations. The aerofoil angle (or angles) can also be adjusted.

Gurney-flaps can be added to rear aerofoils to increase downforce at all types of circuit, except one-mile ovals. At the larger ovals and the Superspeedways, where there are severe regulatory curbs on the sizes of the front and rear aerofoils, Gurney-flaps are a way of clawing back as much downforce as possible.

It is necessary to find an optimum *combination* of settings between the aerofoil angle and the amount of Gurney, because there is a trade-off between downforce (very desirable) and drag (very undesirable, because it can sap speed). For example, setting an aerofoil at a relatively steep angle and running no Gurney is less efficient than setting a shallower aerofoil angle and running a small Gurney.

Like the front aerofoil endplates, the rear aerofoil endplates channel the airflow for maximum efficiency by preventing it from 'spilling out' from the ends of the aerofoil elements and diminishing their effectiveness. The endplates are composed of two skins of carbonfibre sandwiching a layer of Nomex honeycomb (Nomex is a patented product from DuPont containing Kevlar). The rear aerofoil assembly is mounted directly onto the gearbox casing via two vertical struts.

The front and rear aerofoils work in concert. For races on Superspeedways, for example, the rear aerofoil assembly is set to generate the maximum downforce achievable within the narrow bounds of the regulations, then the front aerofoil assembly is set to balance that out.

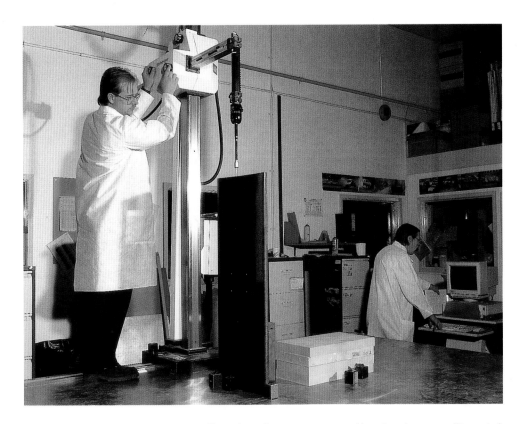

At the end of the manufacturing process, all aerodynamic components are subjected to rigorous quality-control checks – as are other elements of the car. As part of these checks, very precise measurements are made with a three-axis digitiser on a surface table to ensure that each component is absolutely true.

Pictured here is a 'Handford Device' rear aerofoil being precision-measured prior to installation on a car. This high-drag aerofoil was recently introduced to curb speeds on Superspeedways.

At California's Fontana Superspeedway in 1997, Brazilian driver Mauricio Gugelmin achieved a pole-grabbing qualifying speed of 389.91 kph (242.333 mph) in his Reynard-Mercedes – easily the fastest Champ Car qualifying speed ever recorded. Gugelmin's staggering lap highlighted a problem which had vexed CART for some time: the governing body had been seeking to formulate an antidote to the ever-escalating speeds of Champ Cars on Superspeedways amid increasing concerns for the drivers' safety.

Finally, in 1998, CART mandated the introduction of a special high-drag rear aerofoil assembly. This was the 'Handford Device' – named after its designer, Dr Mark Handford, the Technical Director of Champ Car manufacturer Swift. The new aerofoil proved an instant success. On its maiden outing, the US 500 at Michigan Speedway, lap times were indeed trimmed – by around 20–25 kph (12–15 mph) per lap – and, better still, the quality of the racing was buoyed by virtually non-stop jostling for the lead. Drivers found that, with the high-drag rear aerofoil impeding their progress on the long straights every time they tried to 'go it alone', the art of slipstreaming assumed renewed importance.

As drivers sought to slingshot past one another – often four abreast – lap after lap, it was clear that the 'Handford Device' represented a win-win situation for all concerned.

chapter 4 ENGINE & TRANSMISSION

THE REGULATIONS place very severe limitations on the format of Champ Car engines. There used to be an 'equivalency formula' which permitted an alternative engine format (stock block, push-rod, 3.43 litres), but that was rescinded in 1994. Now, all engines must be of the dual overhead camshaft type and turbocharged; the maximum capacity is 2.65 litres (161.71 cu in), and methanol is the only permissible fuel.

Champ Car engines typically produce just over 800 hp at 15,000 rpm. By comparison, Formula 1 engines – which have a maximum capacity of 3 litres (183.07 cu in), and are normally aspirated and petroleum-fuelled – produce up to 770 hp at 17,500 rpm.

CART regulations stipulate that Champ Car engines cannot have more than eight cylinders. In view of the maximum permissible capacity, there would be no benefit to building a four- or six-cylinder engine in any case, because the pistons would be inefficiently big and heavy. The V8 format is therefore universal.

The tight limitation on the number of cylinders – Formula 1 engines, by comparison, are permitted to have as many as twelve, although ten is currently universal – is a measure designed to contain costs, because it reduces the number of moving parts and thereby limits complexity.

Champ Car engines have dry-sump lubrication, electronically controlled injection, and electronically controlled distributorless ignition (CDI).

Champ Car engines are limited to a single turbo unit in order to maintain a check on performance and complexity. The turbo air inlet is mounted on the right side of the engine cover, and is protected from foreign object ingestion by a wire-mesh guard. Turbos are purpose-built for Champ Car engines by specialist manufacturers such as Garrett, and run at speeds in excess of 80,000 rpm.

CART places a regulatory limit on the intake manifold pressure (turbo boost pressure), and the permissible level has been reduced considerably over recent years in an effort to curb speeds. The current boost pressure limit is 40 inches of mercury (40 in Hg is 1.35 bar: this is an absolute pressure, so it is 0.35 bar above atmospheric).

Known informally as the pop-off valve, the boost regulator takes the form of a tower positioned atop the plenum chamber, and is clearly visible protruding from the top of the engine cover. If the pressure inside the plenum rises above the stipulated level, a valve at the top of the tower lifts and pressure is lost. The valve closes again when the plenum pressure has dropped sufficiently, restoring the status quo, but the driver is disadvan-

taged, because the performance of the engine degrades considerably and takes some time to recover. Furthermore, if the pop-off valve activates whilst the driver is negotiating a corner, the handling is unsettled and the car becomes very twitchy.

For these reasons, engine manufacturers go to great lengths to ensure that pop-off valves are not activated, and it rarely happens.

The pop-off valves are supplied by CART, and are calibrated for absolute uniformity. At each race, the teams are allocated their pop-off valves, which are sealed (wire-locked) shut in order to prevent tampering. Lottery-fashion, the teams draw a ticket and collect their pop-off valves from the waiting line. They are observed by CART inspectors as they fit them to their cars, and again as they remove them after the race. This is the only policing necessary, and it has proved to be a highly effective self-regulating system – at least from the mechanical point of view.

From the fiscal standpoint, however, it is another matter. Whilst reducing the permissible boost level appears on the surface of it to be a simple and inexpensive antidote to the ever-escalating performance of Champ Cars, the harsh truth of the matter is that any adjustment to the boost level alters other parameters in the engine performance. There is therefore a strong motivation for manufacturers to make compensatory adjustments to their engines – and it is perfectly legal for them to do so – and this can create an entirely *new* wave of cost escalation. For example, if a manufacturer wishes to go to the ultimate length to re-optimise engine performance in response to a reduction in boost, it may go as far as altering the bore/stroke ratio – and that certainly isn't an inexpensive exercise ...

Over the past few years, Champ Car engines have become lighter, more powerful and higher-revving – despite the fact that the maximum permissible turbo boost level has been reduced considerably over that period, and the regulations limit the use of performance-enhancing materials in engine construction.

Reciprocating and rotating components may not be manufactured of carbon, ceramic or metal-matrix composite (MMC) materials. Only ferrous alloys may be used in the manufacture of flywheels, fasteners and connecting rods. Pistons may only be manufactured from monolithic aluminium alloy, and the only components which can be made from titanium are the valves (which benefit from the lower mass) and the valve-spring retainers and keepers.

Pneumatic valve control – universal in Formula 1 – is prohibited in Champ Car racing. The maximum number of valves permitted per cylinder is four, and camshaft operation must not include a mechanism to vary the valve timing.

The four engine manufacturers currently participating in Champ Car racing – Ford, Honda, Mercedes and Toyota – have seen their respective fortunes fluctuate as first one manufacturer, then another, has gained the competitive edge.

Because CART is owned collectively by the teams themselves, it naturally wants the series as a whole to prosper and therefore only admits engine manufacturers on terms that are conducive to that objective. To prevent an engine manufacturer from 'cherry-picking' one top team, then concentrating all of its resources to establish total dominance to the detriment of the championship as a whole, CART regulations require them to supply their engines to a minimum of five teams, representing at least seven cars. That is, of course, provided there is sufficient demand.

This requirement is waived in the case of engine manufacturers entering the championship for the first time: a policy intended to encourage new entrants. Recognising the fact that the workload is especially high at that initial stage, the governing body requires new entrants to supply only a single car

until such time as their engine becomes 'competition proven' by CART's preset criteria; namely, by qualifying in the top four on the starting grid, or by leading at least 25 per cent of the laps in a race, or by finishing a race in the top five. In the first season after this status has been achieved, the engine manufacturer must supply a minimum of five cars – again, provided there is sufficient demand – then in subsequent seasons, the full 'five teams/seven cars' obligation applies.

Unlike Formula 1, in which engines are often supplied free of charge as part of sponsorship arrangements, Champ Car teams must obtain them in a straightforward commercial manner: they are leased under an 'all-in' arrangement which includes maintenance. Furthermore, engine manufacturers are not permitted to favour one team over another when it comes to supplying engines incorporating development parts. Thus, new-specification evolutions are distributed even-handedly among the engine manufacturer's customers.

There is also a mandatory ceiling on the cost of Champ Car engines: no engine may cost more than ten per cent more than the average price of all of the engine types fielded in the preceding season.

Honda's Champ Car engine – shrouded from prying eyes here – has achieved many successes. Honda is also a major force in Formula 1, with an illustrious past and an ambitious future. Honda's Champ Car engine programme is the responsibility of Honda Performance Development in Santa Clarita, California.

TECHNOLOGY OF THE CHAMP CAR

Reducing the rate of development by limiting technology in Champ Car engine construction has generally proved most effective in controlling cost escalation. However, in certain respects, the opposite effect is achieved. For example, by prohibiting pneumatic valve control, CART effectively forces engine manufacturers to fit steel valve-springs – thereby mechanically constraining rpm – but these can be something of an Achilles Heel in the gruelling race environment, and the engine blow-ups caused when they fail often prove very costly.

Of course, there are two sides to every story. If pneumatic valve control were permitted, the top part of the engine would undoubtedly survive at higher revs, but the simplistic 'steel valve-springs versus pneumatic valve control' argument is not actually the issue. As with most aspects of regulation, the 'steel valve-spring rule' represents a compromise, because if rpm levels were permitted to rise above the current level by the introduction of pneumatic valve control, the cost saving would be short-lived. For while it is generally accepted that pneumatic valve control would increase reliability at the top of the engine, and therefore reduce costs, *higher* costs would be incurred further down the engine, because the limiting factor mechanically would then be the pistons, conrods and so forth, and a whole new spiral of cost escalation would ensue.

Despite CART's best efforts to contain costs, designers are constantly striving to wrest more performance from their engines, so costs inevitably are rising slowly all the time. At the premises of the engine manufacturers in England, the United States and Japan, vast arrays of state-of-the-art automated machining tools attest to the fact that propelling a modern Champ Car is an *expensive* business.

Champ Car engine designers are only too aware that the engine alone does not win a race – it is the overall package of car and engine working in harmony. And it is not simply outright horsepower which singles out a superior engine, because that is only one of several key performance parameters which must be perfected. Of equal importance is the 'driveability' – the ability of the engine to be tractable in a race situation.

The *installation* of the engine in the car must also be perfected – partly due to the role the engine plays in the overall weight-distribution of the car, but particularly due to its influence on the aerodynamics at the rear of the car. Engine designers make strenuous efforts to keep the engine as compact as possible, so that it leaves more room for the system of tunnels at the rear of the underbody which generates so much vital downforce.

Structurally, too, the engine plays a vital role in the overall effectiveness of the car. Like their Formula 1 counterparts, Champ Car engines are cantilevered out from the rear wall of the chassis as a fully stressed structural member – carrying the gearbox, to which the rear suspension and rear aerofoil assembly are in turn attached – so it must be very strong and rigid to cope with the enormous structural loads, yet also extremely lightweight.

The engine is mounted as low on the chassis as possible, to help maintain the car's low centre-of-gravity.

Fuel economy is another vital factor in engine design. A thirsty engine consumes more time on pitstops, forces more restrictions on race strategy, and imposes a greater weight penalty (by necessitating a heavier fuel load).

Finally – and, most importantly of all – the engine must be *reliable*. An engine alone cannot win a race, but it can most certainly lose one ...

Every engine is tested on a dynamometer after being completely rebuilt between races. A rebuild takes approximately 60 hours. An engine typically has a 965-km (600-mile) 'life' before being returned for rebuild. In addition to testing rebuilt engines, dynamometers are used in the relentless drive to develop modifications which give better engine performance.

Whilst the engine manufacturers work ceaselessly to make their engines more powerful, power output is only one factor in gaining a racetrack advantage. It is the car's *aerodynamics* which play the biggest part in making it go faster – especially around corners, where downforce is so important – and also the compound of the tyres. An increase in engine power often makes only a fairly marginal contribution to the overall speed of the car through the course of a race, whereas an increase in aerodynamic efficiency can make a very major contribution.

This was graphically illustrated between the 1996 and 1997 Champ Car seasons, when about 100 hp was sapped from the engines as a result of a further restriction on turbo boost pressure – yet the cars were travelling around two seconds a lap *faster* than they ever had before, due to the increases in aerodynamic efficiency achieved by the chassis designers and the improved compounds developed by the tyre manufacturers.

The point was illustrated even more spectacularly by the massively powerful push-rod engine developed by Ilmor for Mercedes for the 1994 Indianapolis 500 race, which had around 200 hp more than the other engines, yet only bestowed a tiny increase in lap speed. The real benefit of all that extra power was that it facilitated easier overtaking.

One of the challenges of designing and building a Champ Car engine is catering for the enormous speed-range encountered during the course of a season. The racetracks visited by Champ Cars over the course of a season range from street circuits such as Belle Isle Raceway in Detroit, with a high proportion of second- and third-gear corners and an average race speed of around 180 kph (110 mph), to Superspeedways such as Michigan International, with peak speeds as high as 385 kph (240 mph). On a typical lap of Belle Isle, a car will spend 20 seconds in second gear, 28 seconds in third, 12 in fourth, 6.5 seconds in fifth and 11 seconds in sixth.

On some of the highly banked circuits, the driver will want to apply full throttle for the whole of the lap in

qualifying, and also at certain stages during the race, so the designer has to ensure that the engine can withstand the strain of running wide open for a high percentage of the time. Surprisingly, though, of all the circuits visited by Champ Cars during the course of a season, it is the street circuits which account for the highest number of engine breakages.

In the punishing regime of oval racing, reliability at sustained high rpm is obviously crucial – yet at the same time the engine must have torque characteristics which provide 'driveability' on street circuits, where pulling-power out of slow corners is just as important as flat-out speed. Engine designers aim to achieve a very flat torque curve, because even on highly banked circuits where astronomical speeds are maintained consistently, the cars must still be capable of accelerating cleanly away from slower speeds during the rolling start and periods of running under the yellow flag, and accelerating away from a standstill after a pitstop.

The engine has to be equally capable of pulling from very low down the rev range when the car is exiting the low-speed corners encountered on street circuits, or after the driver has been held up in a traffic jam into such a corner. It must allow the driver to accelerate cleanly out of slow corners, tiptoe around them when the track conditions are treacherously wet, and jockey for position when he is surrounded by other cars and his ideal racing line has been compromised.

As a guide, one engine manufacturer claims a maximum torque level of 340 feet-pounds at 11,000 rpm.

Champ Car engines have a pitlane speed-limiter function programmed into their engine control units (ECUs), to ensure that the mandatory limit is not exceeded. There is also a maximum rev limit programmed in, in the interests of reliability – although this can be increased slightly for qualifying.

This spectacular photo captures the moment of engine failure. The most common causes are breakages of the forged aluminium alloy pistons, the machined alloy steel conrods, and – inevitably, given that the engine manufacturers are constantly striving to increase rpm – the steel valve-springs. In addition, the conrod bearings at both ends, and the main bearings of the alloy steel crankshaft, are all potential weak points.

In this particular case, the engine expiring is a Toyota – designed, manufactured and prepared by Toyota Racing Developments at premises in Costa Mesa, California and Aisen Seiki, Japan. Toyota is unique among the current Champ Car engine manufacturers in eschewing Formula 1.

The chassis pictured here is a Reynard. The Bicester, England-based manufacturer's venture into Champ Car racing has been like a fairy tale. It won on its maiden outing – in Michael Andretti's hands at Surfers Paradise, Australia in 1994 – and has gone on to score multiple consecutive championship victories. Now that Adrian Reynard's cars outnumber the others on the Champ Car grid by a ratio of almost four-to-one, he is set to enter Formula 1 as a cornerstone of the new British American Racing 'superteam'.

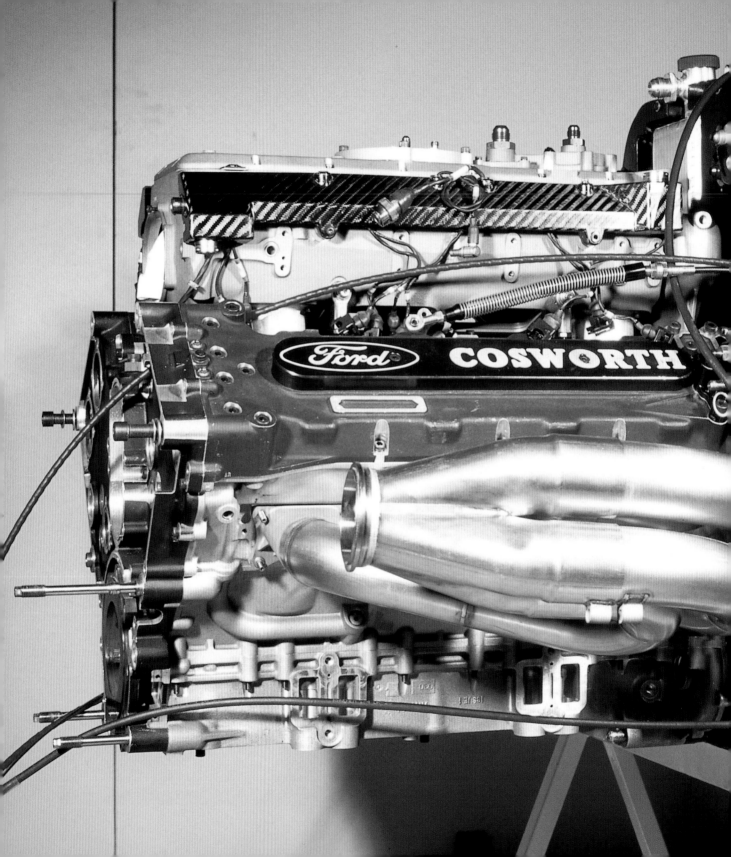

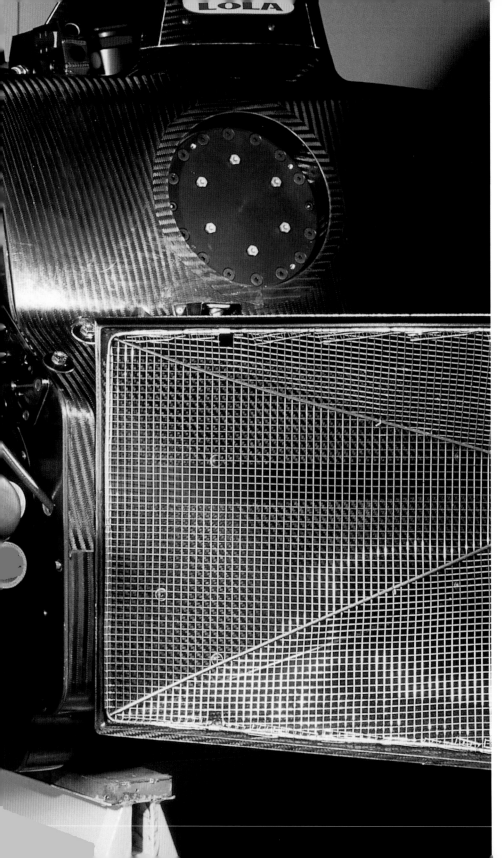

ENGINE & TRANSMISSION

This view highlights the way the Champ Car engine is cantilevered out from the rear face of the chassis as a fully stressed, load-bearing member. Although Honda's first Champ Car engine had a cast-iron block, all of the current engines are manufactured almost totally from aluminium.

The primary structural requirements of the engine are lightness and rigidity. Lightness can be achieved by reducing the thicknesses of the material in the engine block, but if this is overdone it will compromise the other half of the equation – rigidity – because even minute flexing would interfere with the very fine tolerances of the moving parts: for example, by deforming the cylinder liners.

It is essential to achieve a sturdy and secure mounting of the engine to the chassis. The engine is usually joined to the car by a pair of steel or titanium studs on the sump, and either one or two mountings on each camcover.

A Champ Car engine typically weighs 124 kg (275 lb), minus the clutch.

Pictured is the current Ford Champ Car engine. Ford has a long and meritorious history in Champ Car racing, scoring its 300th victory at Mid-Ohio in August 1998 with Mexican Adrian Fernandez (Reynard) at the wheel. Its engines are designed, built and developed by its Cosworth Racing division in Northampton, England. The Ford/Cosworth partnership is also a major player in Formula 1.

The art of packaging – designing the engine so that its size and shape conform as closely as possible to the chassis designer's requirements – is much more important today than it was a few years ago. A very significant factor in this is the need to provide the chassis manufacturer with as much space as possible for the underbody tunnels, due to their vital role in generating downforce.

   Over the past few years, Champ Car engines have become smaller as designers have striven to keep the external dimensions of the block very compact, and the installation of the ancillaries neat and tidy. An extreme example of this trend is the achievement of hitherto unprecedented compactness with the current Mercedes engine. The external dimensions of the 1997-model Mercedes (pictured above) were fairly typical for a Champ Car engine – at 561 mm (22.09 in) long, 555 mm (21.85 in) wide, and 599 mm (23.60 in) high. But the 1998-model Mercedes (pictured right) set new standards and astonished the opposition – at 466 mm (18.34 in) long, 550 mm (21.6 in) wide, and 560 mm (22.04 in) high.

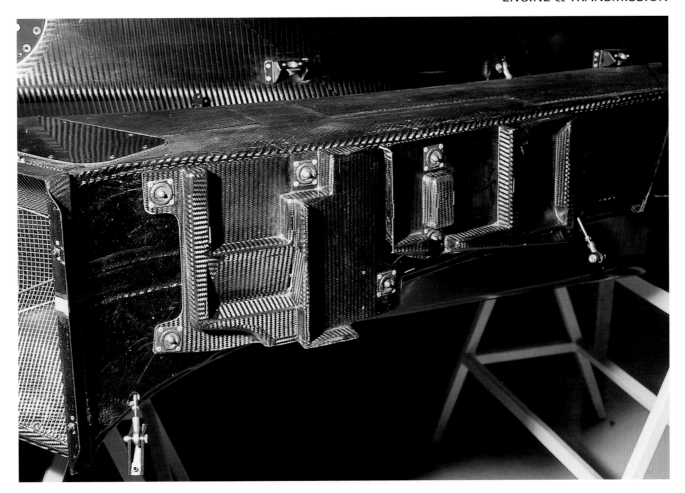

The angle between the cylinder banks is frequently changed, sometimes even season by season, as engine designers seek to improve the packaging. Factors influencing this angle include alterations to the port shape (achieving a smooth flow of gases along the tracts between the turbocharger plenum chamber and the cylinder heads is critical to engine performance) and repositioning of the ancillaries, many of which can be located in and around the vee between the cylinder banks.

Key ancillaries situated in the immediate vicinity of the engine are the water pump, alternator, centrifuge, oil pump, (oil) scavenge pumps, oil filter, and turbo wastegates (there are two: one per cylinder bank). The ECU and other engine-management 'black boxes' tend to be mounted within the sidepods, on the outer surface of the radiator ducts – where there are lightweight carbonfibre brackets to accommodate them. These brackets incorporate rubber mountings to insulate the delicate electrical components from vibration.

The turbo is mounted between the engine and the gearbox, and is – to quote one leading engine designer – 'a nightmare to package'.

Mercedes' current Champ Car engine has an 82-degree angle between the cylinder banks. The British-based engine specialist Ilmor Engineering – headquartered in Brixworth, near Northampton – is responsible for the design, manufacture and development of the Mercedes Champ Car engine. The Ilmor/Mercedes partnership extends into Formula 1, where it has powered the McLaren team to glory in 1998.

Engine cooling is accomplished by water radiators mounted within the sidepods – one on either side, typically served by a single pump. The engine oil is usually replenished from a tall, narrow aluminium tank set in a recess in the rear face of the chassis: this brings weight forward, reduces the pipework, and keeps the oil a judicious distance from the heat of the turbo. The engine oil is cooled, again via a single pump, by either a single water/oil heat exchanger mounted behind the water radiator in one of the sidepods and laid flat so that it doesn't impede the flow of air through the sidepod, or – in the case of the Reynard – an air/oil radiator, again mounted in one of the sidepods.

Wire-mesh guards are mounted in the radiator ducts to protect the delicate radiator cores from foreign object damage.

At the design stage, the engine manufacturer provides the chassis manufacturer with data relating to the engine's water and oil cooling requirements, so that the radiators can be sized accordingly: oil and water flow requirements vary appreciably from one engine/chassis combination to another. In some cases, this is a particularly complex business. The Reynard chassis, for example, is designed to accept all four engine types – Ford, Honda, Mercedes and Toyota – so compromise in the installation of the engine in the chassis is unavoidable. Penske, on the other hand, only designs for the Mercedes unit, so no such compromise is necessary.

Chassis manufacturers construct wooden mock-ups of the radiator layout prior to implementing final construction. The radiators are tailored to the chassis manufacturer's requirements by specialist suppliers such as Serck Marston and Calsonic.

The methanol fuel that Champ Car engines run on itself has cooling properties. These engines burn huge quantities of methanol, and as it evaporates it dissipates heat.

There are contingencies if things get *too* hot. CART regulations stipulate that there must be at least one port sited on the top or side of the engine cover to receive an external pressurised water fire-extinguisher. As a minimum requirement, the piping from this port (or ports) must direct water to the turbocharger and the exhaust system. In addition, the car has its own on-board fire extinguisher system.

TECHNOLOGY OF THE CHAMP CAR

The desire for fuel economy is a very major factor in Champ Car engine design – providing teams with the greatest possible flexibility for their pitstop strategy. Sometimes, if fuel economy is good, it is possible to miss out a pitstop altogether – some oval races can be undertaken with just a single pitstop – and this can heavily influence the result.

There is a regulatory aspect to fuel economy, too. CART regulations promulgated at the start of the 1997 season stipulate that cars must achieve a minimum of 1.85 miles per US gallon. A formula which takes into account such factors as the inside and outside circumferences of the circuit, and the number of warm-up and race laps, determines a precise quantity of fuel which CART allocates to each team at the start of a race.

CART regulations specify that all of the fuel must be contained in a single cell, situated aft of the seat-back bulkhead, and that the capacity of the cell must not exceed 132.49 litres (35 US gal). Due to the nature of the regulations governing their construction, Champ Car fuel cells are far less flexible than their Formula 1 counterparts – which can be inserted through a relatively small aperture in the rear face of the chassis – so Champ Cars have an aluminium bulkhead/firewall there which must be removed to allow the cell to be installed. This bulkhead incorporates a central aperture corresponding with a hatch in the rear face of the cell through which the fuel pumps, filters and collectors may be accessed.

As a precaution against fire, the fuel system must incorporate a 'break-away' coupling between the engine and the chassis to prevent fuel from spilling from the cell in the event of a major accident in which the engine becomes detached.

For obvious reasons, CART imposes very strict regulations on refuelling systems, and inspections are made regularly to ensure compliance. Refuelling may only be undertaken with dry-break disconnect systems approved by CART. Refuelling equipment must be of the gravity type and must not incorporate any kind of pressurisation or vacuum system.

The maximum permissible internal diameter of the refuelling hose is 76 mm (3 in). When refuelling takes place, a second hose is inserted into the top of the fuel cell to take air out (in Formula 1, the refuelling hose performs both functions simultaneously). The end of the hose which attaches to this 'fuel vent tower' has a clear plastic section, so that the mechanic holding it can watch for the moment when fuel starts to rise up the hose – at which point he knows that the tank is full and both hoses are rapidly withdrawn.

A crew member sprays a jet of water at the refuelling valve just before the car departs its pit space, in order to dilute any residual fuel which has splashed out onto the car as the hose was pulled clear.

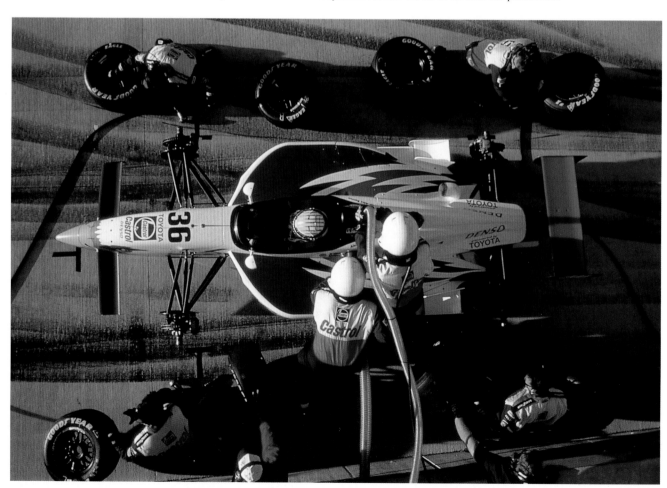

ECATE
Visteon
UTLX 20
Visteon
Duralast
BATTERIES
FedEx
OMEGA BOSCH
Visteo
TURBO
GARRETT
Clausing
Firestone

Weight is a particularly critical factor in the design of the gearbox – because it is sited so far back, and therefore exerts considerable influence on the weight distribution and general handling of the car. In an effort to make the gearbox as light as possible, a designer can be tempted to reduce the casing wall thickness – but if he reduces it too much, major problems will arise when the car has to run. The gearbox will not be rigid enough to prevent it from flexing under the structural loads fed in from the rear suspension and rear aerofoil assemblies, which are mounted directly onto it.

Such flexing would severely degrade the efficiency of the gear ratios within – which run to minute tolerances – and, at worst, could cause the gearbox to seize completely.

As with the engine block, the gearbox casing incorporates webbing and reinforcements to bolster rigidity.

The gearbox pictured here was designed and manufactured by Lola for its 1998-model car. Lola has 'come back from the dead' after a shrivelling Champ Car order book – the legacy of Reynard's shining success – and a disastrous foray into Formula 1 almost put the company out of business in 1997. Motorsport entrepreneur and property magnate Martin Birrane came to the rescue and is steadily rebuilding Lola from the ground up, concentrating on its core markets as a mass-producer of Formula 3000 and Indy Lights cars, developing fresh opportunities, and slowly restoring the confidence of customers.

Birrane is investing huge sums in equipping Lola for the future. For example, he has committed £4.5 million to establishing a purpose-built windtunnel at the company's Huntingdon, England headquarters.

At one time, almost every Champ Car on the grid was a Lola. Only a blinkered optimist could expect those heady days to return, but the expertise to field a winning car – and the will – is certainly there.

All of the current Champ Car gearbox casings are cast. Some are cast from magnesium, because it is lighter than aluminium, but aluminium is generally stiffer and copes better with the heat generated by the turbo, so most manufacturers prefer it. After casting, the gearbox casing is extensively machined by complex CAD/CAM processes – as pictured here.

In the past, some manufacturers have opted to *fabricate* the gearbox casing in an effort to reduce manufacturing lead-times and increase stiffness and lightness. Casting consumes time because of the need to fashion complex patterns beforehand.

The latest gearbox manufacturing method – carbonfibre construction, pioneered by the Stewart and Arrows teams in Formula 1 in 1998 – is prohibited in Champ Car racing on the grounds that its adoption would prompt a major cost escalation. Carbonfibre offers certain theoretical performance benefits: potentially even greater stiffness, lightness and compactness for the gearbox casing.

Gearboxes provide a good example of the difference in technical approach between Formula 1 and Champ Car racing. While Formula 1 cars have semi-automatic gearboxes operated by high-pressure hydraulics or pneumatics via paddles mounted on the back of the steering wheel, Champ Cars must have a wholly mechanical gearshifting system.

However, in common with their Formula 1 counterparts, Champ Car gearboxes are sequential.

All of the current Champ Cars have six-speed gearboxes. For races on ovals, due to the characteristics of the circuits, fifth and sixth gears are almost identical. For example, the Homestead circuit has a fairly constant wind blowing down the two long straights, so the driver selects fifth gear along the into-the-wind leg, and sixth gear when the car has rounded the 180-degree bend to travel in the opposite direction.

Having closely matched fifth and sixth gears also provides extra 'urge' for overtaking manoeuvres and spreads the gruelling workload between two ratios.

A single reverse gear is a mandatory requirement, and the capability to reverse must be demonstrated during scrutineering – except in the case of races on ovals, when reverse gear can be taken off in the interests of weight-reduction. While Formula 1 cars are required to have a drive-disengagement system activated by a button in the cockpit, so they can be removed more easily if they are abandoned at the trackside, Champ Cars are not. Consequently, they can get stuck in gear, so it is sometimes necessary for recovery crews to hoist the rear wheels clear of the ground when towing cars to safety.

The vast majority of Champ Cars – namely, the Reynards – are fitted with a transverse gearbox with internals made by Xtrac of England. However, the longitudinal format lends itself more readily to incorporation in a narrow gearbox casing, thereby allowing extra space for the underbody tunnels, so that has found favour with Penske. The 1998-model Penske has a particularly narrow gearbox, also with internals purpose-built by Xtrac. In both cases, the gears are clustered *ahead* of the rear axle line, where their mass – within the wheelbase – improves the car's weight distribution.

With up to ten steel or titanium studs, the gearbox is joined to the engine via an intermediary structure known as the bellhousing, which houses the clutch and – in some cases – pipework for the turbo. There has been a trend towards integrating the gearbox and bellhousing into a single unit in the interests of weight-saving and structural rigidity. This is the case on the current Reynard, but on the Penske and Lola the bellhousing and gearbox remain separate units.

The mountings between the engine and the gearbox, and/or the bellhousing, can be susceptible to the high heat levels generated by the turbocharger, even though the turbo is heat-shielded. Thermal expansion can feed considerable stresses into these mountings, giving rise – *in extremis* – to breakages: typically, either shearing the attachment studs or breaking the camcover. Thermal expansion generated by the turbo can also affect the preloads of the shafts within the gearbox.

The gearbox oil must be capable of performing well in an exceptionally punishing environment. Gearbox oil temperatures can reach around 125 degrees C, and components would start to lose their hardness – induced by the tempering process (case-hardening) during manufacture – if temperatures rose any higher.

Pressures between the gear teeth are phenomenal. At any given moment in time, virtually the entire motive power of the engine is being transmitted through a fingerprint-sized area of gear tooth surface – and, theoretically at least, metal never touches metal: contact is limited to the oil film.

Gearbox oil cooling can be accomplished by either routing the gearbox oil through the engine water cooling system (Penske has experimented with this), or by the more usual method of mounting a small, dedicated oil/air radiator in one of the sidepods.

Champ Cars are restricted to wholly mechanical differential systems: another sharp contrast with Formula 1 practice. Provided they mimic the behaviour of a known mechanical differential – so as not to be a form of automatic traction control – Formula 1 cars can be fitted with hydraulically actuated, electronically controlled differentials incorporating load-measuring sensors which constantly measure the torque generated by the driveshafts and make adjustments to the drive according to a pre-programmed regime.

CART regulations – in common with those for Formula 1 – stipulate that differential settings can only be changed by the pit crew, not whilst the car is in motion.

Most Champ Cars have Salisbury-type differentials (a little-used alternative is the 'viscous diff', in which plates rotate in a thick, sticky fluid), but on ovals almost all of the cars run with locked differentials.

Continuously variable transmissions (CVTs), which allow the engine to maintain peak efficiency at virtually all times, are not permitted – although there is no doubt that they would be ideally suited to oval circuits.

The driveshafts, and the constant-velocity joints at their extremities, cope with enormous forces and have evolved considerably over recent years. They have become lighter and more compact as a result of improvements in both materials and design, and a steady shift away from the use of proprietary parts to purpose-made components.

Champ Car clutches are not electro-hydraulically activated like Formula 1 clutches, but wholly mechanical. Some are actuated by cable, others hydraulically. The overwhelming majority of Champ Car clutches are supplied to the teams by the UK manufacturer AP Racing. AP supplies three different specifications of clutch (pictured right) for use with the current four engine types: Ford, Honda, Mercedes and Toyota. The American company Tilton manufactures a single type of clutch, compatible with the Ford and Honda engines.

Due to the phenomenal revving capability of Champ Car engines, clutch plates rotate at speeds as high as 15,000 rpm (in the case of the Honda engine) and can be subjected to temperatures as high as 400 degrees C when the driver accelerates away from his pit space during a race.

Carbon clutch plates are prohibited in Champ Car racing. The driven plates are copper-plated steel with sintered-on friction surfaces. Sintering is a process which turns a powder into a solid material by the application of intense heat and pressure.

Like many other components in Champ Car racing, clutches have become ever smaller and lighter. A typical unit weighs just 2.8 kg (6.2 lb), has a maximum external diameter of less than 140 mm (5.5 in), and has four driven plates 115 mm (4.5 in) in diameter, three intermediate plates, and one main pressure plate.

The driver brings the engine revs up as high as 13,000 rpm when leaving his pit space, providing the most stressful test of the clutch in the course of a race. The parts most vulnerable to overheating are: the steel intermediate plates, because the sintered-on friction material can detach or degrade; the pressure plate, which can distort badly, making it difficult to get into gear; and the diaphragm springs – made of steel – which can lose some of their clamping load, although this seldom proves terminal.

chapter 5 BRAKES

BRAKES are a key contributor to the phenomenal performance of Champ Cars. When entering their pit spaces during a race, the cars can decelerate from 96.5 kph (60 mph) to a standstill in 2.64 seconds – so the accelerative prowess of the engine is more than matched by the decelerative muscle of the brakes.

Deceleration forces under braking at some circuits peak at 3.3 G, at which point the wheels lock up – as pictured here – a situation to be avoided, as tyre damage can occur.

Champ Cars can decelerate from 320.2 kph (199 mph) on a long straight to 98.15 kph (61 mph) for a slow corner in just 155 metres (510 feet) and 2.7 seconds. When attaining such performance levels, friction between the discs and pads can generate temperatures of 750 degrees C or more. The discs can even be seen smouldering dull red, then turning bright orange, at certain points on circuits where extremely heavy braking is required, such as Road America, Surfers Paradise and Laguna Seca.

By the end of a particularly gruelling race, some drivers have worn the brake pads right down to the back plates.

When the calipers grasp the discs, the strain on all of the components is immense. The regulations stipulate that Champ Car discs must be made of ferrous alloy, except for races on Superspeedways – Michigan and Fontana – where CART permits carbon-carbon discs. For circuits where ferrous alloy discs are mandated, cast-iron is the universal choice. Carbon discs are more durable than their cast-iron counterparts, and they perform more efficiently at higher operating temperatures.

Champ Car brake discs must have a minimum diameter of 279.4 mm (11 in), and are typically 328 mm (12.92 in) in diameter. The thickness of the disc varies according to the type of racetrack – whether it is a street circuit, road circuit, one-mile oval or larger oval/Superspeedway – but is generally in the 26–30 mm (1–1.18 in) range. CART regulations stipulate that the minimum disc thickness is 8 mm (0.5 in).

With cast-iron discs, the first few laps – until the discs become 'heat-conditioned' – are critical. Iron discs are often run on a machine up to 600 degrees C prior to being supplied to teams in order to 'pre-bed' them, aiding reliability. If an iron disc overheats, it can distort or even crack. By the same token, carbon discs are not immune to the effects of overheating: they can explode spectacularly if their temperature limit is exceeded.

To help cool the brakes, strategic points are ventilated by ram-air directed by carbonfibre ducts which protrude into the airstream. These cooling ducts are not permitted on the *front* brake units – one of which is pictured here – in races on Superspeedways.

BRAKES

Champ Car brake units are currently manufactured by three companies: Brembo of Italy, and AP Racing and Alcon of the UK. Each unit has up to 12 pistons: two pistons per pad, with between four and six pads. The majority of calipers are made from metal-matrix composite (MMC) materials, while the majority of pads are made of a proprietary material tradenamed Carbon-Metallic, which is composed of various carbon-metallic materials sintered together.

The piston and pad areas are specified in CART regulations.

Champ Cars must have two separate brake circuits, to ensure that if one circuit fails the other will still act on at least two of the wheels. To help avoid locking one pair of tyres under heavy braking, drivers can adjust the brake balance between the front and rear wheels from the cockpit via a cable-operated system. Under normal conditions, a little under 60 per cent bias is placed on the front brakes. Because the front brakes do the most work, the rear brake units are sometimes smaller.

Anti-lock and power-assisted braking systems are outlawed, as they detract from the drivers' display of skill.

Pictured here is a rear brake unit, complete with cooling duct.

chapter 6

SUSPENSION, WHEELS & TYRES

VERY highly developed tyres, in concert with highly evolved aerodynamic devices, are the key contributors to the astronomical cornering performance of modern Champ Cars. The tyres are of radial ply construction and are tubeless.

Inevitably, compromises must be made in the design of a racing tyre. For example, while it must be as light as possible in order to reduce unsprung weight and maximise road-holding, it must also be strong enough to withstand the enormous forces imposed on it. Similarly, it has to generate as much grip as possible, yet it must have durability and offer consistent performance.

Although they play a crucial role throughout the race, the tyres tend only to become a focus of attention during pitstops. Television images of pit crews changing tyres with amazing speed and precision highlight the fact that Champ Car racing is a *team* sport.

Like the brake pads and discs, the tyres only operate at full efficiency when they have reached the correct working temperature: normally around 125 degrees C (257 degrees F) at the tread, but potentially as high as 178 degrees C (350 degrees F) under maximum loading while cornering at high speed on a Superspeedway. Cars can unexpectedly veer off the racetrack on cold tyres after a period of running under the yellow flag if the driver does not properly maintain their temperature. The electrically heated shrouds in which Formula 1 tyres are wrapped to bring them closer to their optimum temperature and pressure prior to the car being driven are outlawed in Champ Car racing.

To minimise variables in the set-up, the quality of the air in the tyres is carefully controlled. The air is processed through special equipment linked to the compressors used to inflate the tyres, which converts it into a nitrogen-rich, moisture-free gas. This ensures that each tyre retains constant inflation properties regardless of when it was inflated, and that pressure variations due to changes in temperature are uniform. The high temperature build-up in racing conditions can result in a pressure increase of as much as 7 psi. For this reason, the teams set the pressures so that they are at the optimum when operating at the high race temperatures.

Varying the tyre pressures is one of the methods used to alter the handling of the car. On street circuits and road circuits, operating pressures are lower than those of most road-going car tyres, but on ovals the opposite is true.

The car pictured here is resplendent in the distinctive livery of the All-American Racers team, owned by motorsport legend Dan Gurney. The Santa Ana, California-based team campaigned a Reynard throughout 1997 and for the first half of 1998, but then it sprang a surprise by fielding its own chassis. The Eagle marque has a long and chequered history in both Champ Car and Formula 1 racing, dating back to the 1960s. The 1998-model Eagle was the work of former Formula 1 designer Gordon Kimball.

The 'weight' on a tyre due to the combined effects of the weight of the car, aerodynamic forces, and cornering, braking and acceleration forces is known as the tyre loading. When a car is cornering, the loading on the outside tyres increases and the loading on the inside tyres decreases as the car's weight shifts laterally. The stiffness of the sidewall construction is a very important factor in the tyre's cornering performance, because this directly influences its responsiveness to the driver's steering inputs.

For races on ovals, the tyre construction incorporates stiffer sidewalls to compensate for the increased tyre loadings resulting from the combination of higher speeds and banked corners producing high G-loadings.

Weight distribution also has an important influence on the performance of the tyres. The car's heaviest components are unavoidably concentrated at the rear, placing a greater weight burden on the rear tyres: typically, a Champ Car's weight is distributed 40 per cent on the front tyres and 60 per cent on the rear tyres. Also, while the front tyres only have to cope with cornering and braking forces, the rear tyres must generate tractive effort as well so they have more work to do.

CART's stance on front tyres contrasts with that of Formula 1's legislators. The regulations governing Formula 1 permit the front tyres to be just as wide as the rear tyres. Although no team has yet gone so far as to run identical tyre widths front and rear, there has been an increasing tendency in Formula 1 to fit progressively wider front tyres to increase their share of the workload.

There are two tyre manufacturers in Champ Car racing: Akron, Ohio-based Goodyear, which brands its tyres as Goodyear Eagles – as it does in Formula 1 – and the Japanese manufacturer Bridgestone/Firestone, which brands its tyres as Firestone Firehawks.

Although the teams are specifically contracted to either Goodyear or Firestone, CART regulations require both tyre manufacturers to bring sufficient tyres to each race to supply up to 50 per cent of the grid. They must transport to each race all of the equipment necessary to fit the tyres to the wheels, inflate them, balance and demount them. They also bring computer equipment which undertakes stock control and relays engineering data to the main computers at their respective headquarters for further analysis.

Technicians assigned to each team by the tyre manufacturers are kept busy throughout a Champ Car race meeting. One ongoing task is to monitor the state of the tyres every time a driver comes into the pits. The temperature and wear information they record provides a vital guide to the performance not only of the tyres, but also of the chassis and suspension. This data may also identify a change in the characteristics of the circuit, which may have undergone resurfacing work since the last time it was visited by Champ Cars.

Unlike Formula 1's legislators, CART continues to permit slick tyres for dry-weather running. Because slicks have no tread pattern, they are often – incorrectly – described as 'treadless' tyres. In fact, the tread simply lacks the grooves which form the tread pattern of all wet-weather tyres. The reason for the smooth tread on a slick is that it creates the maximum possible contact area with the racetrack surface within the dimensional limitations set by the regulations.

As one can imagine, the G-forces acting on the tread are massive when the tyre is revolving at over 3000 rpm at top speed.

CART regulations stipulate that, within prescribed tolerances, the front tyres must be 647.7 mm (25.5 in) in diameter, and 304.8 mm (12 in) in width. The rear tyres must be 703.58 mm (27.7 in) in diameter for races on road circuits and street circuits – for races on ovals, 685.8 mm (27.0 in) – and 406.4 mm (16 in) in width.

Unlike Formula 1, in which two different types of dry-weather tyre are supplied for free practice – a 'prime recommendation' tyre and an 'optional' tyre (the latter is generally a softer compound) – after which the teams must choose which type each car will qualify *and* race on, in Champ Car racing there is only a single dry-weather tyre available from each manufacturer. An option is only offered on rare occasions, if CART agrees that

there is 'just cause' – for example, on safety grounds, if a problem has developed with the prime tyre. This is a measure designed to limit the speed escalation which has inevitably resulted from the developmental 'tyre war' between the two tyre manufacturers.

Over the course of a race weekend, they are obligated to supply each car with seven complete sets of dry-weather tyres for races on road circuits, street circuits and short ovals – except 300-mile races on ovals, for which nine sets must be supplied – and 14 complete sets for races on Superspeedways. Tyre manufacturers can also supply what are termed 'stagger' tyres for races on ovals: the right-rear tyre has a slightly larger diameter than a conventional tyre, while the left-rear tyre has a slightly smaller diameter. Because all of the oval races are run in an anti-clockwise direction, these special tyres help the car to turn left (in the same way that a conical object – if pushed – will turn, while a cylindrical object will travel in a straight line).

The difference in diameter between 'stagger' tyres and their conventional counterparts is very small: between 25 and 45 hundredths of an inch, depending on the circuit.

For safety reasons, competitors are not permitted to race on ovals when the track surface is wet. At street circuits and road circuits when the track surface is wet, the Chief Steward may declare the race a 'dry start' or a 'wet start'. For the former, competitors may elect to start on slicks or wet-weather tyres. For the latter, competitors have no choice but to start the race on wet tyres, of which there is only a single type from each manufacturer: intermediate tyres, as used in Formula 1, are prohibited (as are special qualifying tyres). In either case, once the race has started, if the conditions alter, competitors are free to change to whichever tyre they think appropriate.

Wet-weather tyres have a similar construction to slicks. The grooves in the tread are designed to disperse as much water as possible, allowing the tread to grip the racetrack surface. Front and rear pairs of wet-weather tyres have different tread patterns, to suit their different roles.

The aim when designing a wet-weather tyre is to ensure that it will operate efficiently across a wide spectrum of conditions, ranging from a damp to a partially flooded racetrack. The tyre must therefore be capable not only of removing whatever water is encountered, but also of maintaining its temperature so as to sustain optimum performance from the tyre compound. The tread pattern is crucial in this respect.

Overheating can cause a tyre to deteriorate rapidly, and wet-weather tyres are particularly susceptible to this if the track surface dries out too much. In order to prevent their wet-weather tyres from overheating, drivers often seek out the puddles on a drying circuit by avoiding the 'tram lines' which emerge when cars have cleared standing water or moisture from the conventional racing line. Because their aerodynamic underbodies are more efficient than those of Formula 1 cars, Champ Cars tend to dry the racing line more rapidly.

Wet-weather tyres are often 'directional', which means they can only be used in one direction of rotation due to the nature of the tread pattern or construction. They may also be 'asymmetrical', meaning that the tread patterns of the left and right tyres are handed (they are mirror images of each other).

Tyre manufacturers are obligated to supply each car with four complete sets of wet-weather tyres.

Along with the tread pattern, the composition of the tread – the compound – plays a crucial role in determining the level of grip (adhesion) the tyre will generate, and also plays an important part in determining the tyre's wear characteristics. The four basic ingredients are rubber polymers, carbon blacks, oils and curatives.

There are four distinct 'breeds' of tyre in Champ Car racing, to suit the four different types of circuit visited during the course of a season: street circuits, road circuits, short ovals and larger ovals/Superspeedways.

For races on Superspeedways, the compound should be 'heat-resistant' to cope with the phenomenal speeds, and should have good traction and wear characteristics. For races on short ovals, the compound should primarily offer good wear-resistance, in order to cope with the constant high loadings (there are no long straights to temporarily 'unload' the tyres). For races on road circuits, the over-riding requirement is for a compound which will offer good traction in the 'stop-start' environment of mixed fast and slow corners, and wear-resistance is also important (this tyre is very similar to those used in Formula 1). Finally, for races on street circuits, the three most important requirements can be categorised in order of priority as 'grip, grip and more grip' – even to the point of sacrificing some wear characteristics to achieve that.

Although the grip itself is generated at the contact patches between the tyres and the racetrack surface, the driver senses the level of grip through his hands and feet – and the seat of his pants!

An important factor in winning races is conserving the tyres. The driver's actions, or the racetrack conditions – or a combination of both – can cause sufficient damage to the surface of a tyre to severely degrade its performance. Common problems are graining, which is a 'tearing' of the tread surface generally caused by excessive lateral grip, and blistering, which is caused by overheating of the tread compound.

As well as preserving their tyres, drivers must be aware that – when making or attempting passing manoeuvres in the latter stages of a race – the hot, sticky treads will be accumulating a coating of small chunks of discarded rubber deposited off the racing line. The agglomeration of old rubber on the tyres is termed 'pick-up', and diminishes their grip. The rear tyres are particularly susceptible, because they are prone to collect such debris when the driver accelerates hard exiting corners and the back of the car steps out.

Locking up tyres by applying the brakes too hard can also severely degrade their performance.

The forged magnesium alloy wheels – which must be 381 mm (15 in) in diameter – are supplied to the teams by proprietary manufacturers such as BBS and OZ. The mandatory front rim width is 254 mm (10 in), while the mandatory rear rim width is 355.6 mm (14 in).

Although CART-approved wheel nut locking devices must be installed as a safety precaution, wheels can break off in a major impact – and can even, on rare occasions, clear the debris fencing. An otherwise excellent US 500 race at Michigan Speedway in August 1998 was tragically marred by the death of three spectators, struck by an errant wheel from the Reynard of Mexican driver Adrian Fernandez. The right front rear wheel/tyre assembly, with some of the suspension elements still attached, vaulted the debris fence and plunged into a packed grandstand at Turn Three.

In the wake of this accident, renewed attention was turned to the problem of flying wheels, and the height of the debris fence at Michigan was extended.

Unlike their Formula 1 brethren, Champ Cars are fitted with on-board jacks. These 'airjacks' are activated by compressed air pumped into a valve situated on the top of the engine cover, just behind the fuel vent tower. Only six crew members are allowed over the pit wall during pitstops, so the same crew member who handles the air-removal hose used for refuelling also handles the airjack pipe.

During pitstops, the driver helps his pit crew to get the wheels on and off by keeping his foot on the brake pedal.

A maximum speed limit is imposed in the pitlane throughout practice and qualifying sessions, and during the race itself. Unless otherwise specified, the maximum permissible speed in the pitlane is 96.5 kph (60 mph). Penalties are imposed on drivers exceeding this limit by more than 8 kph (5 mph).

CART regulations do not permit the use of composite materials as structural load-bearing components – except in the case of the chassis, the bodywork, and the aerodynamic devices and their associated supporting structures. Therefore, the use of composite materials for suspension components – widely adopted in Formula 1 as a weight-saving measure – is prohibited, and steel is *de rigueur*.

The major external suspension elements are the upper and lower wishbones, and the pushrods which convey the forces to and from the inboard shock-absorber/spring units. At the outer extremities of the four suspension assemblies are the uprights. An upright is typically fabricated from steel and serves as the interfacing joint connecting the wishbones and pushrod to the axle/wheel-bearing assembly and brake unit (and, in the case of a front upright, the steering arm).

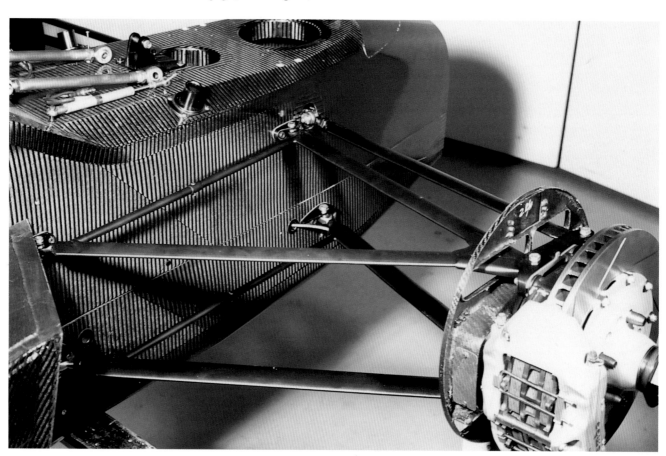

The shock-absorber/spring units are mounted internally to tuck them away from the airflow, reducing aerodynamic drag. They are connected to the pushrods via rocker mechanisms. At the front, they are mounted on the top of the chassis - in front of the cockpit - covered by a carbonfibre hatch; at the rear, they are mounted atop the gearbox, shrouded by the engine cover.

An ability to set up a car effectively - undertaking the complex process of adjusting the aerodynamic devices, suspension geometry and tyres to optimise the handling for the driving conditions on a specific circuit - is one of the crucial skills separating success and failure in Champ Car racing. The aerodynamic factors in achieving a good set-up are inextricably linked to the mechanical factors.

The better-equipped Champ Car manufacturers - such as Reynard - test the dynamic performance of the suspension on a static test rig in the comfort of their headquarters. The car is mounted on a complex system of hydraulics which imposes loadings duplicating those fed into the car on the racetrack. The hydraulics are commanded by software downloaded from previous runs on specific circuits and captured on the car's on-board instrumentation. The static test rig can simulate, for example, the loads which are fed into the front and rear suspension in high-speed corners, including the bumps in the racetrack surface. Braking and acceleration loadings can be fed in simultaneously - and aerodynamic loadings can also be fed in, either independently or simultaneously.

chapter 7 THE COCKPIT ENVIRONMENT

ALTHOUGH not strictly a 'technology' item, the driver is a vital element in the functioning of a Champ Car, so it is only proper that we include him and his working environment, the cockpit.

The phenomenal performance of these cars places enormous physical strains on the driver. Lateral forces of up to 4 G can be experienced through high-speed corners, and vertical forces can reach 2 G on heavily banked corners. Such G-forces are truly punishing over a race distance.

Forces of acceleration and deceleration are less severe than those experienced in a Formula 1 car, due to the fact that Champ Cars are heavier and have inferior braking performance. Nevertheless, the driver's neck muscles must react to almost constant fore-and-aft forces as the car rapidly gathers speed out of corners or viciously erodes speed under braking into corners.

A driver's vision can be impaired by the high G-forces encountered during hard cornering, as the flow of blood to the eyes is affected by such forces, deteriorating peripheral vision and distorting perspective. Severe bumps in the racetrack surface can also be disorienting: although Champ Cars are less stiffly sprung than Formula 1 cars, high vertical G-forces can momentarily drain the blood from a driver's eyes, impairing his vision.

THE COCKPIT ENVIRONMENT

With such massive forces bearing upon them, it is little wonder that Champ Car drivers must maintain obsessive fitness regimes to stay competitive. Their neck muscles must be developed to counter the high lateral and longitudinal G-forces, and their arms and hands must be muscular enough not only to cope with those forces, and with the vertical G-forces imposed by bumps and undulations in the race-track surface, but also to turn the steering wheel when the 'weight' of the car has risen under the influence of high aerodynamic downforce levels at higher speeds, making the effort of steering more strenuous.

The human heart normally functions at 60–80 beats per minute, but at qualifying and race speeds a driver's heart-rate can soar way beyond that. During qualifying for a Superspeedway race, several drivers' heart rates were measured as an experiment. Going into the first corner, one driver's heart rate was 165 beats per minute, and it peaked at 185 beats per minute during the course of that lap. Heart rates as high as 208 beats per minute have been recorded during Champ Car qualifying sessions. Such rates could be fatal to a person not totally fit.

The driver's overall fitness and stamina must be developed enough to maintain strength and concentration throughout a race lasting as long as three hours. To make matters worse, the high temperatures experienced at certain races – where cockpit temperatures can soar to 50 degrees C – are exacerbated by the multi-layered fireproof garments the drivers wear. Dehydration also contributes to fatigue. Drivers sip energy-giving drinks during pit stops to help replenish some of the lost liquid and vitamins, and some adorn their nostrils with the patented stick-on plastic devices favoured by athletes to open their air passages and thereby aid breathing.

Fire is not the hazard that it used to be in Champ Car racing, but the risk is still taken very seriously. The drivers' overalls are composed of multiple layers of a lightweight flame-resistant material. The layers – and the stitching – are a weave of Nomex fibres.

CART regulations refer drivers to the FIA's regulations for racewear. These stipulate that an 800-degree C liquid propane flame be blasted onto a section of fabric for 12 seconds to verify its flame-resistance. This test results in severe damage to the outer layer, but protection is such that the inner layer sustains only moderate scorching. In actual fact, the overalls will protect the driver for around 30 seconds against direct flame penetration.

Under their overalls, Champ Car drivers wear a long-sleeved rollneck Nomex vest: a few wear 'long johns' for extra protection. In an accident, the knees, elbows and ankles can be subjected to painful knocks within the confines of the cockpit, so many drivers fit additional padding to those areas. Their Nomex gloves have extra padding to guard their knuckles, and suede palms to protect against blistering and improve their grip on the steering wheel. For fire-protection combined with dexterity on the foot pedals, the drivers wear Nomex-lined suede boots over their fireproof socks. Under their CART-approved crash helmets, they wear a Nomex balaclava.

CART technical inspectors examine the drivers' protective garments during scrutineering, and can also undertake random spot-checks after races.

For comfort – and style! – drivers' overalls are custom-made, but they are also highly functional. For example, the epaulettes are specially reinforced, so that the driver can be pulled from the cockpit if he is incapacitated in an accident.

CART regulations stipulate that the driver's seat must be constructed of an approved energy-absorbing material, and that the driver should be situated as far aft and as close to the seat-back bulkhead as possible. An all-important seat fitting ensures that the driver is fully supported in the car against the massive cornering, acceleration and deceleration forces he will experience, by creating a form-fitting seat profiled to his own unique body shape.

The seat-fitting takes place at the team's workshops. A large plastic bag is placed in the cockpit, then the driver climbs in and sits on it. The top of the bag is held open to allow an equal mix of two chemical agents to be poured in. From the moment they are blended together shortly before pouring, these two agents begin a chemical reaction that creates a foam-like substance which expands within the bag and then solidifies, conforming exactly to the driver's contours.

Whilst this chemical reaction is in its final stages, the driver must maintain what he feels is a comfortable position in the car, supporting himself until the foam begins to harden, and then – at the critical point as he feels the foam solidifying – uses the bag as a seat, allowing it to support him. When the bag is removed, excess foam is trimmed from the edges, then the seat is given several coats of resin to harden it further, ensuring it will withstand the rigours of race-track use.

Driver vision is a vital consideration when the car is designed. The quality of the driver's view forwards is vitally important for obvious reasons, but his view backwards is also critical – both from the standpoint of racecraft and safety. Unless he has an awareness of the relative positions of his opponents' cars, he cannot adequately defend his racing line. Worse, he may pose a hazard to faster cars.

The sizing and positioning of the rear-view mirrors are therefore critical, and both are governed by the regulations. These call for the reflective surface of each mirror to have a minimum depth of 51 mm (2 in) and a minimum width of 108 mm (4.25 in). The mirrors are slightly convex to increase peripheral vision – and, as can be seen in this view of Andre Ribeiro, the edges of the reflective surfaces are slightly curved. Even the radii of these curves are specified in CART's regulations book.

Champ Car steering wheels often bear many of the key switches, instruments and displays, although these can also be sited on the cockpit rim or on the dashpanel immediately behind the wheel. Dashpanel manufacturers – most dash displays are made by Pi Research of the UK – will tailor the instrument layout to suit the team's and driver's requirements.

The instruments are almost exclusively digital, and there is usually a primary LCD which can be programmed to display whatever information the driver wishes. Typically, that includes engine rpm and oil pressure, fuel-state and gearshift position. There are also warning lights which illuminate when a temperature or pressure goes out of bounds, and there is often a separate LCD array comprising a row of lights which illuminate in rapid succession in synchronisation with the rpm to 'cue' the driver for a gearshift.

Champ Car steering wheels are made of aluminium. They must be rapidly removable to provide adequate clearance for the driver to climb from the cockpit in an emergency, or be lifted out if he is incapacitated. A lever behind the steering wheel is pulled back, allowing the wheel to be pulled off the spline at the top of the steering column.

CART regulations specify that the steering wheel hub must be padded with a resilient material not less than 9 mm (0.75 in) thick.

Because Champ Car gearboxes are sequential, it is virtually impossible for the driver to miss a gear. A conventional gear lever is situated on the right side of the cockpit: jabbing it forwards changes down, pulling it back changes up. The gear lever activates the gearshift ratchet mechanism via cables.

This is all in sharp contrast with Formula 1 cars, which have gearshift 'paddles' mounted immediately behind the steering wheel which allow the driver to change gear via electronics and hydraulic actuators without so much as lifting a hand. Such systems are prohibited in Champ Car racing.

Close to hand, just above the gear lever, is the brake-bias adjuster: a knob, turned clockwise or anti-clockwise, which allows the driver to alter the comparative braking effort between the front and rear wheels to help avoid locking one pair of tyres under heavy braking. Another key cockpit control is the adjuster for the anti-roll bars – or 'sway bars' – pictured here. By moving these fore or aft, the driver can either stiffen or soften the front and rear suspension roll characteristics, altering the car's handling.

By using another control, the driver can adjust the fuel mixture. Yet another control provides a full-rich mixture and raises the threshold on the rev-limiter, allowing the driver to squeeze more power from the engine – provided there are sufficient fuel reserves. Termed 'pressing the button', this contingency can generate an extra 300–400 rpm for a final dash for the chequered flag, or to pull out a commanding lead or undertake a crucial passing manoeuvre.

The cockpit environment takes on a somewhat stark appearance in this view of a car under construction – with the seat, steering wheel and instrument panel yet to be fitted.

For lightness and precision, the steering column is 'gun-barrelled' from a solid bar of steel. To cater for driver preferences, steering columns are adjustable, and they must be constructed in a manner which will restrict rearward movement in the event of a frontal impact. Steering racks have evolved considerably in recent years, becoming lighter and more efficient as a result of better materials and design, and a shift away from proprietary to purpose-made racks which have much greater resistance to wear. Previously, wear in the rack and pinion during the course of a race introduced unwelcome 'play' into the steering.

Power-assisted steering is prohibited in Champ Car racing.

The throttle pedal is situated on the right side, and has a comparable amount of travel to that of a roadgoing car. Unlike Formula 1 cars, Champ Cars must have a purely mechanical linkage between the throttle pedal and the engine, with no electronic assistance or control. However, as a safety precaution there is a sensor – either a potentiometer or a pressure sensor – which tells the engine management system if the driver has lifted off completely, thereby preventing the throttle from accidentally remaining open.

The brake pedal is situated in the middle, with the clutch pedal to the left. The brake requires a deft touch – but also huge pressure: typically 150 kg (330 lb), generating well over 1000 psi in the brake lines. Power-assisted brake systems are prohibited.

Although two-pedal arrangements of the type seen in Formula 1 are forbidden – there *has* to be a clutch pedal – some Champ Car drivers use the left-foot braking technique. This removes the fractional time-lapse between lifting the foot off the accelerator pedal and locating it on the brake pedal, so it is potentially advantageous if a driver can master it.

The clutch pedal is not used for upshifts, as CART regulations permit a 'shift without lift' function to be programmed into the engine management system to automatically drop the engine revs momentarily the instant the next gear is selected. This 'spark cut' allows the driver to leave his foot flat on the throttle pedal during upshifts, but as it is not permitted for downshifts, the vast majority of drivers use the clutch pedal when changing down – and, of course, for driving out of the pits.

All of the foot pedals are adjustable fore and aft.

Champ Car drivers are strapped firmly into their cars with a multi-point safety harness comprising two shoulder straps, two abdominal straps and two crotch straps. The shoulder straps are heavily padded at the points where they come into contact with the driver's collar bones.

CART regulations stipulate that the straps must be at least 76 mm (3 in) wide, have a minimum tensile strength of 3632 kg (8000 lb) in the case of the lap straps and 1362 kg (3000 lb) in the case of the shoulder straps, and be connected by a quick-release buckle.

To provide additional protection for the driver's head in the event of a major accident, Champ Cars have a 'collar' of deformable padding which extends right around the rear periphery of the cockpit opening. Strict regulations govern the dimensions and positioning of the CART-approved padding material, which must be at least 51 mm (2 in) thick and must extend from the base of the driver's helmet with the driver seated in a normal driving position to within 165 mm (6.5 in) of the top of the rollover hoop.

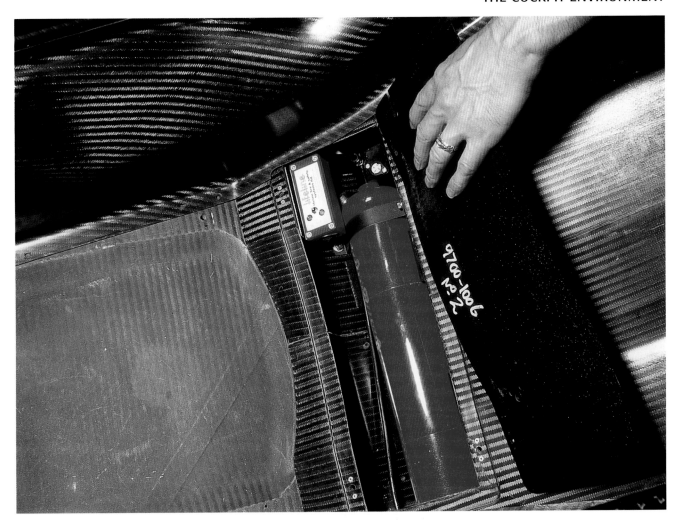

CART regulations stipulate that cars must be fitted with a fire extinguisher system, mounted within the wheelbase (a compartment beneath the driver's seat, as pictured, is an ideal location). It must be capable of being activated both by the driver – by means of a button on the dashpanel – and externally. AFFF is an acceptable fire-extinguishing agent: dry powder-type extinguishant is not.

The minimum weight of the charge must be 2.27 kg (5 lb), and the system must direct extinguishant at the most probable areas where fire could occur – for example, the oil coolers, and the fuel and exhaust systems. It must not, for obvious reasons, spray extinguishant directly at the driver.

Although it is not a mandatory requirement, CART regulations recommend that cars be fitted with a life-support system consisting of a medical air bottle and fire-resistant pipe for connection to the driver's helmet. The bottle for this system must be positioned within the wheelbase, within the chassis structure or otherwise protected from impact.

To protect against the risk of fire or electrocution in the event of an accident, CART regulations decree that the driver must be able to kill the car's electrical circuit by means of a spark-proof circuit-breaker switch on the dashpanel. Its position must be marked by a master switch identification triangle. In addition, an external cut-off switch – which takes the form of a D-shaped handle located on the right side of the rollover hoop – must be operable from a safe distance by a pole with a hook in an emergency.

This handle has a dual purpose, because it also serves as the external activation switch for the car's fire-extinguisher system. Its location, on the left side of the race car at the base of the rollover hoop, is denoted by a circular *E* (for 'Extinguisher') symbol.

Both in the pits and out on the racetrack, the driver can communicate with his team via a two-way VHF radio link. Here, team owner Roger Penske is pictured discussing race strategy with one of his two drivers.

The driver wears earplugs fitted with tiny earphones, and he has a small microphone fitted to his helmet, close to his mouth, activated by a button on the steering wheel. The key topic of conversation is race strategy, but drivers also alert their pits to faults developing on their cars.

CART is much more open about driver/pit radio communications than the masters of Formula 1. While Formula 1 teams scramble their radio exchanges to prevent interception by rival teams and the media, CART teams allow their transmissions to be relayed live to a worldwide television audience!

Computers, hand-held monitors and a host of other electronic devices play an important role in the driver's relationship with his car, whether he is comparing his lap times with those of his competitors in the tense atmosphere of a qualifying session, or calmly analysing his car's performance between sessions.

The way in which drivers exercised their skills in the cockpit was something of a mystery until the emergence of data-logging and telemetry. Now, all of the driver's inputs through the steering wheel, brake pedal, throttle pedal and other controls can be analysed in minute detail in the pit garage or back at the team's headquarters.

Telemetry is the process by which readings from sensors installed throughout the car are transmitted by radio waves to a receiver in the pit garage, where they are stored on computers and displayed on banks of monitors. A constant stream of information on the engine performance, for example, includes the rpm, oil temperature and pressure, and – vital to race strategy – the fuel flow rate. Data relayed from other key components include the individual wheel speeds, and measurements of the movements of the front and rear suspension assemblies. By monitoring wheel bearing temperatures, teams can warn their drivers of an impending failure and call them back to the safety of the pits. Similarly, sensors mounted on the wheels provide warning of slow punctures.

The transmissions are strictly one-way. CART regulations prohibit the transmission of data to the car in order to prevent teams from telemetering commands from the pits to remotely alter the functioning of the engine and modify other key parameters to improve the car's performance in response to changing conditions out on the racetrack.

Other data-acquisition devices can be carried during testing, but are prohibited at race meetings: lasers for measuring the ride-height and pitot tubes for measuring air pressure.

By dint of their superior performance, all of the data-logging systems used in Champ Car racing are provided by Pi Research.